A Parent's Guide to

Coaching Football

John P. McCarthy, Jr.

BETTERWAY PUBLICATIONS, INC.
WHITE HALL, VIRGINIA

Other titles by John P. McCarthy, Jr.:

A Parent's Guide to Coaching Baseball
A Parent's Guide to Coaching Soccer
A Parent's Guide to Coaching Basketball

Published by Betterway Publications, Inc.
P.O. Box 219
Crozet, VA 22932
(804) 823-5661

Cover design and photographs by Susan Riley
Photographs by Cathy Cimato
Typography by Park Lane Associates

Library of Congress Cataloging-in-Publication Data

McCarthy, John P.
    A parent's guide to coaching football / John P. McCarthy, Jr.
        p. cm.
    Includes index.
    ISBN 1-55870-201-6 : $7.95
    1. Football for children—Coaching. I. Title.
GV959.55.C45M33 1991
796.332'07'7—dc20   91-4063
                                                               CIP

Printed in the United States of America
0 9 8 7 6 5 4 3 2

To Geraldine Capodiferro
Whose love and caring make everyone
feel special.
My mother-in-law, with love.

CONTENTS

INTRODUCTION.. 7

1. DESIRE.. 9
   What is Desire?
   Developing the Right Attitude
   Confidence

2. BASIC SKILLS 17
   Blocking
   Tackling
   Passing
   Receiving
   Running
   Specialties

3. FIELD POSITIONS 61
   What Position Should Your Son Play?
   Offensive Positions
   Defensive Positions

4. WHAT IS FOOTBALL ALL ABOUT? 79
   The Concept of Downs
   Moving the Ball
   Major Rules
   Jargon—Talking Football

5. CONCEPTS, FORMATIONS, PATTERNS 105
   Offensive Concepts
   Defensive Concepts

Offensive Formations
Offensive Play Patterns
Defensive Formations

6. ODDS AND ENDS **127**

Work with Your Child
Boys and Girls?
Conditioning
Injuries
In the Stands
How to Treat the Coach

7. PARENT'S CHECKLIST..................................... **135**

INDEX.. **141**

INTRODUCTION

"I want to play football, Dad," said my ten-year-old son Joe. He had been thinking about it for a year or so and had now decided to go for it. I knew that he had begun to sense the glory of the game, the popularity, the cheerleaders. I hadn't urged him to play football, as I did with other sports. One reason was that football started in August, when I usually planned our vacation. I figured he would eventually try out in high school, but admittedly I had some trepidation about his playing before then, particularly while he was in that growth spurt period from ten to thirteen. Let's face it—it's a rough game. I played and was injured a few times, and I've got some old friends who are still hobbling around. I guess there is something instinctive in a parent that gets us worried about a child playing in such rugged competition.

Anyway, he chose to play and my wife and I chose to support his decision. He signed up for a local Pop Warner team. His weight qualified him for the Junior Midgets, 90-115 pounds.

Most of the other kids had already played for a few years, but Joe made the team and started at fullback. I was happy to see the way that Pop Warner rules separated the kids so that they played against other kids in their same age and weight class.

I started to think about how I as a parent could help my son. It occurred to me as I watched him at practice and as I considered the game more carefully that there were dimensions very different from the other major sports. Sure, there are skills that need to be learned, and parents can be *very helpful* if they are knowledgeable about and can explain fully the various techniques and the basic skills of blocking, tackling, rushing, and passing. There are also numerous ways parents could help practice these skills with their child.

There were virtually no books geared for the beginner. That's one problem I hope to resolve with this book. However, the area in which kids seemed to struggle most was in that all-important area of desire and confidence. As I watched, it occurred to me that parents could be most helpful by trying to get their child properly motivated to play the game.

I get sickened by the way some coaches preach violence to the kids, screaming, "Kill him, go out there and hurt someone!" I know that they are usually just trying to psych a kid up, but I can't see how such guidance is good for young boys. I understand that it's an emotional game, but parents need to ensure that their child gets a correct perspective. That's the second reason I wrote this book.

I have learned throughout my life—in sports, in my professional career, and in my family affairs—that at times things can get pretty rough. But just hanging in there, knowing how to get up and just hold on, is sometimes all it takes to make it. I have also learned that tough problems require concentrated effort and reaching down to give it all I've got. And, most important, I've learned that there is always that something extra within me, always there, ready to help out. All sports teach these life lessons, and football perhaps teaches them best of all. It is not about violence; it's just about not quitting. It's about finding that special extra reserve we all have within us. This is the message of football, and it is the third and main reason for this book. If this book does nothing else, make sure that your child gets that message. Help your son find the good in this game, and also help him to avoid the negatives.

Writing books about youth sports has been a most interesting and rewarding experience for me. *The Parent's Guide to Coaching* ... books on baseball, soccer, and basketball have all been quite successful beyond my hopes, and so some kids are surely being helped. That's what it's all about. When writing a book, I find myself more deeply into the inner essence of a sport than when I actually played these sports. Writing this book has given me a new perspective on football, and I hope that by sharing it, you will be able to help your son, as I have learned to help mine.

GO FOR IT!
Jack McCarthy

1.
DESIRE

This is the most important chapter in the book. Don't skip it just because the word *DESIRE* seems obvious or abstract! It is the most important aspect of football for both the player and the parent to understand. Without it your child will probably sit on the bench or play poorly. With it, he will surely find the game an exciting experience. You and your child will hear coaches say countless times, "Football is ninety percent desire!" Believe it!

Desire is the essence of football. If you, as a parent, can find a way to light the fire of desire in your child, you will have helped him in the most meaningful way possible. Watch a game at the younger ages, and you'll see that some of the kids really stand out. They make aggressive tackles or crunching blocks. The better running backs really pop the line, moving low and hard, running almost with an abandon. Other kids are hanging in there, holding their own, giving enough effort to make a decent go of it. Still others seem to be standing around, trying to avoid contact. They are usually not on the field for very long.

The main difference among all three groups is desire. Sure, strength, especially upper body strength, is very helpful. So is speed —no doubt about it! At the high school level they remove the weight restrictions that are in place for grade schoolers, so sheer size then becomes important. But at all levels it is *the desire to mix it up*, to give a good jolt, that separates the players from the substitutes. If you can instill or increase this attitude in your son, he will

Figure 1
DESIRE

The essence of football is the desire to overcome an opponent.

Figure 2
GOOD CLEAN ROUGHHOUSE

Have your child approach the game nonviolently; it's just a romp.

improve his play far more than he could by weight training, conditioning, or learning basic skills.

WHAT IS DESIRE?

By desire we mean *the determination to overcome an opponent*, whether it be by a solid block or by thwarting the block attempt of an opponent and going on to make the tackle. Desire is a state of mind, an abandonment of self, a form of courage, the joy of mixing it up. It is doing one's very best, calling up whatever available reserve power, and not ever quitting. It is playing both for one's self and for the team's interest. It is the exercise of a determined will, flowing from one's competitive spirit, which drives one to achieve his goal. (See Figure 1.)

The good news is that desire is available to all kids. It's not just for the gifted few. Sure, some kids seem to be already fully motivated. However, in others it gets buried under a lack of confidence, or maybe a lack of interest, and so it needs to be dug out a bit and fired up. I believe it can be. We have all seen it happen. The unfolding of confidence in a child is truly a joy to behold. Football is quite different from most other sports. As is pointed out in my other books on parent-coaching, hitting baseballs, or controlling a soccer ball, or shooting a basketball require highly refined skills. Sports such as these require constant practice, repetition, and great concentration. While football certainly involves all of these, and we will discuss football skills in great detail later on, football is nonetheless primarily a game of strength and rugged body contact. The key to football is more in the desire to overcome the individual opponent than in the development of individual skills.

DEVELOPING THE RIGHT ATTITUDE

The good news is that parents clearly can help to bring forth this attitude. It takes communication and talking over certain concepts with your child.

If your child is already highly motivated, then there may be little need to increase his desire. He has already won over half the battle, and the joy of the game will be his. However, particularly at the very young ages, most youngsters are at least a bit hesitant about the game and so they can greatly benefit from some parental communication. Talk it over! Here are some approaches to consider.

It's Just Legalized Roughhouse!

Kids love to roughhouse! In fact, adults often have to restrain them for fear of someone getting hurt or breaking something. Well, football is legalized roughhouse! It's quite helpful and positive for kids to look at it that way. It's a chance to go out on the field for a couple of hours and romp and tumble. It's really not about violence or anger, as some coaches unfortunately teach the kids. It's not about "going out there and hurting somebody" as some coaches yell (although, in their defense, most times they don't really mean that, they are just trying to fire a boy up). It's not about getting angry, getting mad, or hating someone. It's just good clean roughhouse. (See Figure 2.) Help your child to understand the difference, particularly if his nature is not very aggressive. We don't want to change their nature, and we certainly don't want to make them violent. We just want to teach them that it is possible to reach down within themselves and bring forth an exuberance, a sense of personal strength, an indomitable pride, and an intensity of spirit.

Some kids shrink from all of the violent talk, so discuss the matter in a straightforward way with your child if he is hesitant or struggling. Tell him that it is just about romping, about pride, about teamwork. It's a fun free-for-all. Yes, he needs to hit hard. Yes, he must concentrate and be explosive, but it's not about meanness. Channel his perception and energy in a positive way and he will respond as if a weight has been lifted from him. He will begin to look forward to the next game with a new fresh purpose. I have seen it happen!

Your Son is Well Protected

Remember, the football equipment today is quite good. The helmets have a special, scientifically developed lining and completely protect the head. The knees, hips, ribs, thighs, shoulders, and often even the elbows are safely padded. (See Figure 3.) Weakness at the ankle, wrist, shin, or neck can be further protected with tape, wraps, or a collar. Neck collars are not mandatory, but I recommend you buy one if one is not issued with the gear. The point

Figure 3
REQUIRED EQUIPMENT

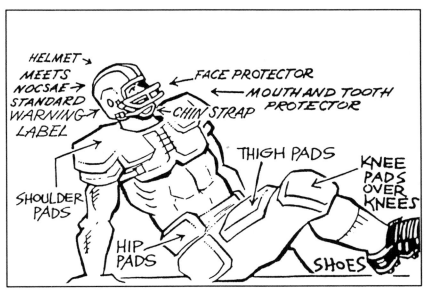

The protection is really quite thorough. Neck collars, elbow and fore-arm pads, and shin guards are not mandatory, but should be worn. (Courtesy NFSHSA.)

is that the kids are very well protected. It's important for your child to understand how well protected he is, since it will lessen any reluctance to really drive or slam into an opponent. The kids are not very heavy in youth leagues, especially in the first several years, and they don't have enough strength or size to really give a crunching lick, so injury is much less likely than in later years.

I've coached and played a lot of sports, and frankly, I've not seen more injuries in football than, for instance, in soccer or basketball. I believe there are two reasons for this; one is the protective gear, and the other is the more rugged conditioning that regularly occurs in football. Tell your child this. Of course, there are no guarantees—it *is* a contact sport. But the protection they have is excellent and they can and should rely upon it.

Most children have a basic fear of getting hurt (don't we all?), limiting their aggressiveness. Fear is usually the greatest obstacle for any young athlete in almost all sports. It's good to point out to your child how well protected he is, and that injuries are rare. Tell your son there is no need to hold back, just go for it!

Never Quit!

Football comes down to one-on-one competition. On any given play, most players on the field are locked in combat with a single opponent. Sure, there is double-teaming and other maneuvers that could require contact with several opponents, but most times it's one-on-one, and often it's against the same opponent for most of the game. Sometimes the opponent will be stronger than your son, sometimes not; it will vary. Usually the coaches will spot a mismatch and stay away from it, or double-team a strong player. But, regardless, your son has a decision to make.

The most important thing to recognize is that there will be times when your son is playing against a stronger opponent, and that no matter how strong the opponent is, if he does his best, he will at least slow him down, and that may be enough. It's okay not to be able to succeed every play! *It's just never okay to give up.* Another teammate may be able to open a bigger hole on the other side, as long as your child can hang in there. So, even if your son is getting beat, he can't quit. He has to give it his best, try to find a weakness, mix up his approaches, try different things, but never quit. A good opponent will usually play well, but there is great pride in knowing that you did your best and, by hanging tough, prevented the good player from completely having his way. It's also consoling for youngsters to know that they are not expected to do what they can't do; they are only expected to do their best and not to quit. More often than not, *just with increased desire alone*, by reaching down for all you've got, you can find a way to overcome the obstacle. That's a great life lesson! If you discuss this with your son, he may just give it a shot.

Play Until the Whistle

Often a kid will stop when the play goes away from him, such as to the opposite side of the field. Nothing looks worse to the coach than a player standing still and watching the action (particularly if the game has been filmed). Your child must know to always continue until the whistle blows. Go hit somebody, run towards the play, stay animated — do anything except stand and watch. This attitude helps to keep his desire up. It will also help keep him free of the coach's anger. Moreover, every once in a while, the play will reverse back toward him, and in that case continued effort will have been quite important to the team.

CONFIDENCE

Confidence is a most elusive quality. Football is a sport that builds it. The coaches yell and bark a lot, kind of like the military, but the idea is to get the kids to wake up. Your child will get yelled at and will be upset by it. It's okay! You will be worried by it and will begin to feel protective, perhaps angry at the coach, but just try to go with it. He's just trying to motivate your child, to toughen him up, to prepare him, and to get him excited enough to put a hard hit on someone. Players often are surprised by what they can really do when they *get riled up by the coach*. Sure, some coaches overdo it, and there are certainly problems if a hostile coach arouses the wrong feelings, but usually it's for the better. Once a kid sees what he can do, he'll keep on doing it. The coach is just trying to get him to the point of giving himself a chance.

The antagonist of confidence is fear. Let's face it, we have all experienced it. Some people live with it daily. It's a part of life. The ability in life to overcome or transcend fear is one of the keys to survival and ultimately a key to happiness. Your child has his own fears, and football will bring him to terms with them. I believe that youth sports in general, and football specifically, act to overcome fears.

A kid naturally worries about trying something new—will he be good enough, will he be able to take it? He finds himself flat on his back a few times, the coach yells, he is embarrassed. He gets back up. He keeps going. In a few weeks, he makes a big play and it starts to dawn on him that much of the problem was just his own fear and self-doubt. He learns that he can overcome these things with determination, hard work, and not quitting. He has found life's greatest friend . . . confidence. I've seen football lead to this, and it's a good thing. Go for it!

2.

BASIC SKILLS

There are certain basic skills that must be learned and then must be executed on every single play. Blocking and tackling are probably the most important, since on nearly any given play twenty-one of the twenty-two players on the field are doing either one or the other. Your child must learn how to block or how to tackle, and if he learns both, he may play both ways on both offense and defense. Passing, running, receiving, and pass defense are also major and essential football skills. Then there are specialty skills such as punting, place-kicking, snaps, and special teams.

As mentioned in Chapter 1, the desire to overcome the opponent is of primary importance. However, poor skills can greatly reduce the effectiveness of individual effort. An informed parent can be most helpful in this respect, particularly with regard to proper form. Help your child with the *details* of technique before he develops bad habits that will take years to change.

Often, with thirty or more players on the field at practice, the coach may not notice flaws in each player's form, or he may not communicate clearly to your child the technique and *the concept behind the correct form*. Here is where the parent can help. Focus on your child's form at practice or at a game. Scrutinize his *stance*, the height of his attack, if his legs are digging forward, where the hands and forearms are positioned, how long his effort is sustained, and other areas covered in this chapter. There are some drills you can use to work on form.

Frankly, I think a video tape of a practice, scrimmage, or game is a very effective tool for teaching. I don't think they are used much below high school level to teach the players. Yet, I believe film is an excellent method to review form and execution. I've used it and it works great. Zoom in as close as possible. Then, when you view the tape later, look at my checklist of techniques and review and discuss each one. There may be no better coach than your child's own eyes and his ability to see his errors with your help and correct them himself. Try it; a picture is worth a thousand words.

BLOCKING

Blocking is the attempt to prevent a defenseman from tackling the ball-carrier, preferably by removing him from the path of the ball-carrier, but at the very least by interfering with his ability to tackle. Blocking is done by everyone on the offense, but it is the primary job of offensive linemen, especially the five interior linemen. They are the unsung heroes of the game. Even a defensive lineman will hear his name on the loudspeaker when he makes a tackle, but it's rare that an interior offensive lineman gets public credit for the great block that led to a touchdown. These players must learn to play just for the personal satisfaction of being part of a team and of overcoming their opponent. Sure, there is less glory, but the true fan of football knows that all positions on the field are of equal importance. Running backs know that they live or die based on the performance of their linemen. Linemen do a tough job, and they have to love it. I know—I was one of them when I played.

One day early in the season your son may come home disappointed when he finds out that he has been assigned to a line position. Chances are it's because of insufficient speed. He'll get over it. Don't make a big deal out of it. He is part of a team and should focus on being as good as he can be wherever he is needed.

Often, at the youngest ages the most yardage is gained by a speedster just running wide around the whole pack. This is because the blocking up the middle is often ineffective. The kids are just learning blocking techniques. If you look at the interior linemen, you will see the kids standing straight up, seemingly just leaning on or pushing each other. (See Figure 4.) With such poor blocking form, a hole for the running back is not formed. As the boys mature,

Figure 4
BLOCKING

*These linemen are standing up, and as a result the
runner is about to get nailed.*

Figure 5
READY POSITION

*The ready position, about to descend
into the set position.*

by seventh and eighth grade the blocking is much improved, and dive plays up the middle become more effective. In later chapters, we will discuss blocking as it relates to each position and as it relates to overall offensive strategy. However, the basic techniques for blocking are set forth below.

The Blocking Stance

The whole idea of the correct stance is to give the blocker a good start. Each part of the stance is designed to increase your son's potential to overcome his opponent. He must be able to get low enough so that he can make it *under the opponent's center of force*, which is under his shoulders, and yet still have enough power and balance to jolt the opponent, raise him, and sustain the block. It's a tall order, and good form helps.

1) Ready and set positions. A lineman descends into his "set" position, or blocking stance, from an interim stance, which is called the *down* or *ready* position. (See Figure 5.) After breaking from the huddle where the play is called, he sets his legs a few feet back from the line of scrimmage. The legs are spread about as wide as the outside of the shoulders, with one foot back a few inches. Hands are on the knees, and the eyes are straight ahead. Upon command of the quarterback, he will snap down sharply into the "set" stance, from which he will commence the block. The object of the "ready" position is to ensure that the snap movement into the "set" stance is smooth and deliberate. *Once a lineman is in the set position, he may not move again until the ball is snapped.* Therefore, the movement into the set position must be exact. It is a twofold motion; the back foot drops back a few inches and the hand on that side drops to the ground into a three-point stance. Once the knuckles touch the dirt, the player cannot lift them again without incurring a penalty.

2) Feet wide apart and balanced. In the set stance, a lineman's feet should be spread at least shoulder-width apart. If the feet are too close together, the opponent will more easily be able to shove a blocker to one side. The action in the middle of the line is heavy and a player can easily be hit from the side and knocked off-balance. The toes may be pointed slightly outward for power and balance. However, with legs spread, the blocker has greater lateral balance. The weight mainly rests on the front or balls of the feet. The toes of the back foot are even with the heel of the front foot,

Figure 6
CORRECT STANCE

Tail not too high, back straight, head up, weight moderately forward, legs bent.

Eyes forward, down hand inside back leg, legs spread nicely, coiled.

although this can vary according to the player. Taller players often set the back foot farther back than do shorter players. The back foot should not be adjusted once in the set position, since any movement can be viewed as intention to draw the defense offside. (See Figure 6.) The back foot is the power foot, and it *drives into the strength and thrust of the opponent*. It is also the first foot brought forward for balance and to sustain the block. Theoretically, the back foot should be the right foot for those on the right side of the line and vice versa on the left side, but it is also important to be comfortable and feel balanced. Kids usually drop the right foot back no matter what side of the line they're on. A good drill is to have your son squat with feet in the "set" position and roll around his body weight on them. He can find the foot position that seems to give the best balance for his body frame. This drill also strengthens the lower legs.

3) Three-point stance, weight moderately forward. The hand on the same side as the back foot snaps down to a point on the line just inside of the back foot and just forward of the shoulder. Roll the weight forward; the knuckles are down and the thumb is back. Some kids like to balance on their fingertips, but the knuckles give much more stability. The weight should be moderately forward on the hand, just enough so that the player would fall forward slowly if this hand were suddenly removed. With sufficient body weight forward, the player can get a fast start and build momentum quickly. However, with too much weight forward, the player will not be able to react sharply to defensive movement, particularly stunts. Also, he will not be able to pull laterally if that is his assignment. The other forearm should rest comfortably on the thigh. However, it is not forgotten. It must be poised, fist clenched, ready to drive forward and up into the opponent's chest. The three-point stance is recommended, especially for offensive linemen. It's very tough to pull, trap, cross block, or adjust to stunts from a four-point stance.

4) Back straight, tail down. The idea behind the stance is to create a low, coiled position from which to launch the shoulder forward, under the opponent's shoulder, and to generate enough power to lift and thrust the opponent out of the way. If the back legs are not bent enough, then they will not be coiled with maximum power. Furthermore, straight legs lift the tail up higher than the shoulders and this detracts from the forward thrust, wasting energy in a downward motion. Finally, it is hard to keep the head

Figure 7
INCORRECT STANCE

Head down, tail too high, legs too straight, weight too forward.

Not too bad, but legs a bit too close, down hand outside of back foot, head down a bit too much.

up if the tail is too high, and a lowered head will limit vision. The tail should be even with the back, or even slightly lower, for maximum effect. However, if the legs bend or squat too far then we lose time and effort to straighten them out. Another common problem with the young player is that his back is rounded. This also happens when the legs are not bent enough or spread enough apart. If the down hand is not far enough out in front of the shoulder it can also result in a rounded back. In effect, the player is merely bending down from the waist. It is a very weak position, and *is dangerous since the head is also down too low*. (See Figure 7.) Make sure that the back is straight and parallel to the ground.

5) **Bull the neck, eyes forward.** It is critical to look straight ahead. The defense, especially the linebackers, are *trained to look at the eyes of the offense for clues* to where the play will go. Your son certainly does not want his opponent to know that he intends to block him. The element of surprise is important. It gives an edge to the offense, so don't tip off the defense by looking at the person who will be blocked, or by looking to the side the ball will go to. It is especially important not to lean in the intended direction of the play. A blocker should angle his thrust to the left or right depending on the path of the ball-carrier, but this must not be done before the ball is snapped. A "poker face" is important, so discuss this with your child. Bull the neck, bracing it for contact; keep your head up and chin forward; and give away no clues!

If a player does not bull the neck and instead allows it to tilt or look downward, two things can happen. First, he doesn't fully see the defender and can lose him or have him slide off more easily. Second, he could strain his neck upon contact. Develop the habit of bulling the neck on every play.

The Blocking Charge

1) **Explode with the snap!** The most important moment in blocking is the first split second when the ball is snapped. The offense knows exactly when the ball is to be snapped by the center to the quarterback, but the defense does not know this. The quarterback calls out a cadence of signals and ends with a series of hikes, such as "hike, hike, hike," or "hut-one, hut-two, hut-three." He has already told the players in the huddle which of these numbers will signal the snap.

This is a valuable opportunity. It is the "edge" the offense has

Figure 8
THE CHARGE

The edge: The offense is in motion and the line is charging forward before the defense has even moved at all.

Here the defense (on the right) is out-charging the offense, which is slow and has lost its edge.

—the element of surprise. The blocker can set his angle and charge forward before the opponent moves. He can, particularly if the target is directly in front of him, strike with full momentum before the opponent has a chance to build up any momentum. Therefore, a quick charge at the same instant as the snap can give the blocker a very powerful edge. I don't think that the need for a very, very quick thrust at the moment of the snap is emphasized enough in youth football. You can correct this by talking about it with your son. If he understands the concept and the edge it provides, he will have discovered a powerful tool. I remember thinking about trying to hit my opponent across the line *before he even moved a muscle.* Tell your son to consider this and to try it during practice. It is an approach that will increase his quickness and add to the explosiveness of his initial contact. Even if the opponent is farther away, such as a linebacker or someone in the defensive backfield, a quick move is important. Quickness can be practiced!

2) Drive forward with the back foot. The back foot is the power foot, and it gives the body its thrust and forward momentum. Sure, both feet are used, but the back foot drives the body in the initial direction desired. It's good for a player just to be *aware* of where his power side is. This helps him draw from it.

3) Stay low, legs wide, knees bent. The most common mistake young linemen make, especially at the beginner level, *is to stand up as the ball is hiked.* This reduces the power of the forward thrust and eliminates any chance of delivering a good hard jolt to the opponent. The edge from knowing when the ball would be snapped is also lost, and the blocker becomes vulnerable. All he has is his strength, and the opponent now has an edge since defenders can fully use their hands to shed and shove the blocker sideways. It is important to stay low with the charge and keep the head up and knees driving forward to build up maximum momentum. (See Figure 8.)

4) Forearms rising forward, elbows out. The forearms are aimed for a point under the shoulders, rising forward in anticipation of contact, ready to slam into and raise the opponent's upper body upon contact. The elbows are initially out to broaden the blocker's breadth as much as possible. This helps to hinder the opponent who tries to shoot or dive by to one side or the other.

5) Angle, don't step, to the opponent's side. A common mistake made by blockers is to step initially to one side, trying to cut off the opponent from the path of the ball-carrier. It's a natural move, and I did it myself plenty of times in order to *secure* an angle I needed. However, it reduces the momentum of the forward thrust and also lessens the "edge" obtained from knowing when the ball would be snapped. Overall, it takes away from the *jolt* that can be delivered. It's a trade-off. If I was a lot stronger than my opponent, I preferred to secure the lane and didn't need the jolt since I could still overpower him. But if he was good, then I had to rely more on quickness. Generally, the charge should be straight forward, just angled enough to get your head on the side of the opponent where the ball-carrier will run. As noted below, we want to give the maximum jolt, and then, only after stunning the opponent, do we try to turn and force him away from the play.

6) **Detect and adjust for stunts.** Again, if the charge is quick enough, one can pop an opponent before he gets in gear. However, the blocker needs to pick up stunts and adjust accordingly, particularly if the opponent is not close. If the opponent is slanting to one side, then adjust the thrust. If the opponent is a linebacker, then his stunt may take him out of the play and someone else will need to be blocked. Decisions must be made quickly, and the ability to adjust takes experience. It is important, however, to know which angle the opponent is taking, and to be generally aware of the surrounding traffic.

The Blocking Jolt

I love this word! It really captures the sense and essence of what the blocker should try to do. Ask your son what happens to him when he is jolted himself; how he feels stunned for a second, perhaps even disoriented. Ask him how easy it would then be to move him around. This is how we want the opponent to feel, even if he is distracted for only a split second. A good jolt deflates the opponent's momentum and allows the blocker to stand him up and get deeper into his midsection. Furthermore, it distracts the tackler from finding the ball-carrier and, most important, teaches him respect and makes him more cautious for future plays.

1) **Jolt hard, as low as possible.** If the opponent is head on or just to one side of the blocker, the jolt is the culmination of the charge. *The idea is basically to slam a forearm and shoulder into the opponent as hard as possible.* Sure, we want to be as low as possible and we want to get under the opponent's shoulder. But in close quarters, with only a split second's time, we have to take what we

Figure 9
THE JOLT

The initial contact often decides the success of a block.

Figure 10
SUSTAIN THE BLOCK

This player, legs driving (see arrow), has a nice sustained block into the midsection of the opponent. Head should be up more.

Figure 11
DIG HIM OUT

The defenseman has dropped to all fours so the blocker (see arrow) comes in low to dig him out.

get. Don't sacrifice the jolt for position. A good jolt is a powerful and effective weapon. Smash that forearm and shoulder into the opponent, then worry about what to do next. The ideal is to hit the opponent's upper thigh and drive up into the midsection. But, whatever part of the opponent we hit—often it's the shoulder—the objective is to belt it hard. The concept is to view one's shoulder as a battering ram or as a boxer's punch, and throw it hard into the opponent. If the opponent is farther away, the blocker will have time to dip just before making contact. The dip is like a wind-up that loads up more power, and it also serves to get the body a bit lower before the jolt. (See Figure 9.)

2) Drive, don't lunge. Thrust and bring the back leg up. The initial charge is hard but it is not a lunge. The knees straighten out upon contact. It's important to be under control so that the next move—a sustained block—can be carried out. The eyes must be open. It's important not to turn the head away, for it is possible for the opponent to slide past you. The jolt occurs quickly, and the blocker needs to be under enough control to maintain balance and sustain contact with the defender.

Sustain, Drive, and Turn

1) Maintain balance. Often blockers lunge too hard, or the defender's quick reaction causes the blocker to make contact off center. Whatever happens, it is critical to *keep the legs wide and regain balance* by bringing the back leg forward and under the body. The eyes must be open to assist with balance. Lean directly into the defender's pressure. At all costs, avoid losing balance and falling to the ground. It happens too often, and a player can do little on the ground. If necessary, a block can be sustained by supporting the upper body with a hand on the ground. If the blocker does fall, he must keep blocking from the ground, sliding or crawling into the defender to try in some way to interfere with the tackle.

2) Drive up into the opponent with short, choppy steps and turn him. Once the jolt is delivered, with the legs still wide, drive the defender back with short, quick, choppy steps. Maneuver the body between the ball-carrier and the defender, lifting the defender with the hands and forearms. Keep up constant pressure to interfere with the tackle. Try to turn the defender away from the path of the ball-carrier and then back to the line of scrimmage to prevent pursuit. (See Figure 10.) Keep the legs up underneath the body as much as possible to avoid losing balance.

3) Use the hands, palms out, to shove the defender. One of the most common penalties committed by an offensive lineman is *holding*. This is called as often as *offside*. A defender starts to get by a blocker and the blocker grabs him or wraps an arm around him. The blocker can use open hands, palms out after delivering the jolt to push the defender, as long as the hands are extended and are out in front of the blocker's and opponent's frames. But he can't grab and he can't hold. It's a major penalty—10 yards—and is costly.

Specialty Blocks

1) Trap or mousetrap. It's a lot easier to block a player from the side than it is to block head on. When we block from the side, we avoid all of the opponent's thrust and momentum. Therefore, traps are often set up. The simplest trap is a *cross-block*, in which two blockers who are next to each other cross and block each other's man. Usually the offensive tackle crosses in front of the offensive guard, and then the guard traps the defensive tackle from the side as he crosses the line of scrimmage. The offensive tackle must move out very quickly toward his man and thus get out of the guard's way. The guard pauses and then quickly pivots, charging with strength into the side of the onrushing defensive tackle. This works best when the defender is penetrating quickly, since the blocker can just "ride" him using his momentum and push him out of the path of the ball.

In other traps, a lineman will *pull* to trap a player. Usually a guard will do the pulling, or occasionally a tackle will pull. The target of the trap can be the nose guard or perhaps a defensive end. When pulling, the blocker pushes to the side with his down hand, pivots, takes a small step with the back foot, and drives along the line of scrimmage with the front foot. Of course, this assumes that the back foot is on the same side he is pulling to. The arms pump quickly to get up speed. He must stay close to the line of scrimmage, dip by bending the knees, and with his eyes on the hip of the opponent, dip and give a jolt. If the pulling guard is to lead a play through a hole, he enters the hole, widens the legs, stays low, and anticipates the first defender to come from the inside (usually a linebacker).

If a guard with the right foot back has to pull to the left, then his first step is obviously with the left foot. Again the step is a short one and should be back a bit so as not to be too close to the line of scrimmage.

Sometimes the defender will sense that a trap is coming, and he will have been coached to drop immediately to all fours. If this occurs then the trapper must prepare to *dig him out* by driving into his side or shoulders and trying to turn him or just smother him. The blocker must always play the defender and time the charge to the speed and height of the defender. (See Figure 11.)

2) Quickness is a key. When blocking a player *downfield*, the first job is to get to him as quickly as possible. One must know the path of the ball-carrier. A shoulder block is preferable since it keeps the blocker on his feet. The key to downfield blocking is to stay under enough control to make contact. Often the approach to a defensive back is at an angle, so the idea is to get the head between him and the runner, step in front with the foot nearest the runner, and drive the opposite shoulder into the target's midsection. To repeat, if the runner is to the right and heading around right end, and the defensive back is approaching from the left, the blocker steps out in front of the defender with his right foot and drives into him with the left shoulder. Once you make contact, you ride the defender and simply interfere, slowing him down as much as possible. A well-timed *cross body block* can also be effective. Here the player pivots on one foot, lifts the other leg outward, and turns the body horizontally, driving the hip into the opponent's midsection. Another option is the *crab block*, in which the blocker starts with a cross body block and as he drops to the ground he crab-walks on all fours against the defender's legs.

3) The double-team is often used against a very strong defender. Two blockers simply drive their shoulders into either side of the opponent and drive him back. Another option is the *post and wheel*, in which one blocker hits head on and the other hits to one side, trying to turn the defender away. (See Figure 12.)

4) Finally, there is pass blocking. Here the blocker does not charge, but drops back a step and holds his ground. The feet are churning, and his responsibility is to block the area he is standing in. The blocker lets the defender *come to him!* He looks to pick up any stunts and he jolts the first defender to approach. He keeps his hands in front and his legs churning. The idea is to interfere with and stop the pass rusher, or at least to slow down or turn the defender to the outside. The best technique is to *shiver blow*, driving

Figure 12
POST AND WHEEL

One blocker (the post) hits from the front and the other wheels the tackler around from the side (see arrow).

Figure 13
DEFENSIVE STANCE

Low, similar to a blocker, but weight is more forward for more thrust.

Note the four-point stance of the defenders on the right.

both palms forward and up into the defender's shoulders. Then recoil and shiver again. Pass blocking is much easier than other types of blocking, as long as the blocker keeps his balance, stays on his feet, and interferes with the pass rusher for as long as possible. The desire here is not to overcome the rusher; it is just to slow him down and thus protect the passer.

5) Other blockers. Our focus to this point has been on blocking by linemen. Many of these techniques apply as well to running backs. They often find themselves facing a situation similar to a downfield blocker. On a sweep play, the blocking back needs to get *outside* of the defender if he can. On a play to the right, he must get the right foot out in front of the defender and squeeze the left hand and elbow in front of him also. Then he simply drives into him with the left shoulder. This kind of *open field block* form is also useful for guards when they pull on ends and is similar to downfield blocking form. If the play is designed to cut inside, then the blocker reverses and hits with the outside shoulder, driving the defender outside.

TACKLING

Football is tackling. I believe that tackling is the act that best demonstrates what football is really about. The most tenacious kids on the team will play defense; they will do so because they make tackles. Tackles don't have to be pretty, they just need to stop the ball. Less aggressive kids can play the offensive line, but defensive play absolutely demands desire and the kid who loves the fray. Good tacklers are hard, tough kids.

Tackling is the endeavor to stop the forward progress of the ball by forcing the ball-carrier to the ground. The object is to stop the ball cold, not even allowing the running back to fall forward. The ideal is to hit the ball-carrier hard enough to force him backward, preferably to cause him to lose possession of the ball. A fine crunching tackle will always bring great praise from the fans, the coach, the teammates, and the announcer. Proper form for tackling comes naturally to an aggressive kid. His mind is focused on stopping the ball-carrier, and anyone else is just an obstacle to be overcome quickly. He claws and fights by or through the interference and comes in hard on the running back. There are, however, several concepts and techniques that the beginner should understand.

We will discuss defense in general and the play of individual defensive positions in later chapters.

The Defensive Line Stance

Every single play in football begins with a proper stance. This holds true for each player—offense and defense, linemen, backs, and receivers. Everyone should start each play with a proper stance. Tackling, therefore, also begins with a solid stance, especially for the down linemen. The worst thing for a defender to do (besides getting knocked down) is to *allow a blocker to get a shoulder into his belly*. A good stance is more important to the offensive lineman since he cannot move once he is set. The defensive stance is less rigid, and defenders can adjust, stunt, or change the intended angle of thrust at any time, depending on the situation.

1) Defensive stance. The defensive down lineman's stance is similar to the blocker's. Feet are wide and balanced; weight is moderately forward but significantly more forward than the blocker's; and the back is straight, with the tail down. (See Figure 13.) Stay close to, but not in, the neutral zone.

2) As low as possible. The shoulder should be even with or lower than the blocker's shoulder. As stated before, the worst thing that a lineman can do is rise up too quickly and let the blocker give a blow to his midsection. I always found a three-point stance, with the weight balanced, to be somewhat preferable. A four-point stance may be used, particularly by shorter, quicker players. If a four-point stance is used, the weight is distributed evenly on all fours.

3) One foot back, preferably the inside foot. Since we prefer to bring up the inside foot first so that the lineman can more squarely handle an outside blocker on a sweep or off-tackle run, it is better for the down lineman to keep the inside foot back a bit and step first with it. The ankles can be flared out a bit for more power.

4) Eyes forward, searching for clues. Check the eyes or look for any slight lean by the opponent. Look at the quarterback, running backs, and other linemen. Try to get a feel for the direction of the play. Think about the down and the yardage, and whether a pass or a run is likely. Usually teams won't run the same play twice, so think where they might choose to go next. Valuable clues can be gained. But do not think so much that you *forget to watch the snap* or *fail to react to what actually occurs*.

5) Crouch stance. Standing defensemen like the end or linebacker stand in a crouch, knees slightly bent, inside foot forward, arms hanging to the side, hands waist high, palms out, and weight forward on the balls of the feet.

Hit and Hunt; Shiver and Shed

There are a number of phrases used for the first defensive move. The basic idea is to meet the blocker, neutralize his charge, and move into the pressure to find and stop the ball-carrier. It is critical to keep these first two concepts in mind. *One must hit the blocker to neutralize him, and then recover and shed the blocker.*

A common error is to rise too soon to look for the ball-carrier, or to try to shed the blocker by stepping around him without neutralizing the charge. Instead, it is essential to give the blocker a good jolt of your own. Keep repeating to your son: hit and hunt, shiver and shed, neutralize and move on. Let's go through these steps one by one.

1) **Watch the snap and move quickly upon it.** The defense is not allowed to be in or across the neutral zone when the ball is snapped (although they may retreat back across the line before the ball is snapped as long as they made no contact while offside). It is important to anticipate the snap and explode very quickly upon it. The first move in football is almost always the most important, and quickness is usually behind most successful moves. The quarterback will try to pull linemen offside by varying his cadence, and referees will allow him to do so unless it is flagrant. So, while players must listen to the cadence, and tense up near the time for the snap, it is *the snap that must be focused upon.* The offense knows the count. They have the clear advantage of surprise and so can build up momentum behind their charge and jolt. The defender can compensate for some of this with quickness to minimize the offensive momentum.

2) **Neutralize the blocker's charge.** There are basically two ways to do this: a shoulder charge or a shiver charge. A shoulder charge is used when the idea is to penetrate the defense. Jolt the shoulder, just like in a block, against or under the blocker's shoulder, bring up the forearms to lift the opponent, bring up the back foot for balance, and drive through, using short, choppy steps. Always have the head up, looking for the flow and pressure and searching for the running back. *The key is to stop the blocker's charge and momentum* and thus be in better shape to shed him. A shoulder charge can also be used when no penetration is desired,

Figure 14
CHARGE, SHIVER, AND SHED

This tackler (see arrow) has mounted a fine charge and is bringing arms forward and up to the blocker's chest.

This fellow neutralizes the blocker with a shiver, holds him at bay, and prepares to shed him.

Figure 15
SHED

Hold the opponent at bay with arms out and shed to go for the ball-carrier at the right moment. Here #61 sheds #74 to tackle #21.

such as in a short yardage situation when the defense needs to protect territory. In this case, focus more on neutralizing and then on *lifting* the blocker. (See Figure 14.)

The shiver is used to protect territory by neutralizing and holding the blocker at bay while looking for the ball. It is used more by defensive ends and linebackers, but can also be used by down linemen who want to mix up their approaches. The idea is to *jam the opponent's shoulder pad in an upward direction* with a stiff straight-arm move, palms out, using both hands. Keep the opponent away until the ball-carrier is spotted and then shed him. Again, neutralizing the blocker's charge head-on is almost always preferable to trying to step around him. Such avoidance moves more often expose a player to an easy block from the side. Also, a common error is to rise to look for the ball before having neutralized the blocker.

There are times when a neutralizing charge is not used, such as in a *submarine dive*, a knee-high dive between two opponents during which the defender uses his quickness to penetrate. The key here is to bring the legs up very quickly and do a push-up with the arms to regain a ready position after diving through the line. It works well against taller blockers or blockers who don't stay low. Another quickness play is to *dive over* the top of a very low blocker, arms extended to break the fall, landing on bent legs, crouched and ready to drive. These moves are used particularly by the nose guard to mix up his stunts and keep the blocker off-balance. However, most of the time, a hard neutralizing charge is what is needed. It is the best way to control the neutral zone, and that's what wins ball games.

3) Stay under control. If no blocker shows up, there is no one to neutralize. When a defensive lineman doesn't get blocked immediately, chances are someone is pulling from the line and preparing to trap him from the side. Bells should go off! Slow down, stay under control, drop to the ground, give the trap blocker a forearm or a shoulder, hold fast, and stack things up. Scratch and crawl on all fours toward the ball-carrier, trying to slow him down or stop him. If you only plug up the hole, you at least will force the runner to go around you—hopefully closer to another defender.

4) Recover and shed. When both players receive a jolt, chances are the defender got hit harder due to the blocker's greater momentum. This is why the recovery must start simultaneously with the jolt. Bring the forearms up, lift and begin to push the opponent away, and drive forward with short, choppy steps. Look for the ball and drive toward it. (See Figure 15.)

5) Focus and wrap. Now it's showtime! It's just your son and the running back. Once he has thrust the blocker to one side, he should drop back to a low position, keep moving, and *focus* on the runner's belt. Spread the feet and drive the shoulder into the midsection or upper leg area. Jolt with the shoulder, bring the legs up quickly and the hands together, and clasp the arms tightly around the runner. Then lift and drop him quickly. Sometimes in a running situation, a side tackle, an ankle tackle, a from behind tackle, or a tackle falling in front of the runner is all that is available. Try to get a shoulder into him, but don't be choosy. Muscle him down any way possible—but remember, focus, jolt, and wrap the arms when possible. (See Figure 16.)

When rushing a passer, get the arms high, waving them to obstruct vision or block the pass. Then bring the arms crashing down upon the passer from above. Wrap the arms and hug him to the ground.

PASSING

By the turn of the twentieth century, football was perceived as a brutal and dangerous game. President Teddy Roosevelt insisted that the recently organized N.C.A.A. legalize the forward pass, and this probably saved the game. Modern footballs are now slimmer to facilitate the passing game. In Chapter 3 we will talk more about quarterbacks in general. They do much more than pass, and they require a rare combination of talents. However, to pass they should preferably be tall and have big hands, strong arms, good eyes, full field vision, courage, a knack for knowing when to release the ball, and, of course, throwing accuracy.

In the grade school level there are far fewer passes than later on at the high school level. The pro's nowadays pass about half of the time, yet each youth team will run maybe thirty-five to forty plays a game and throw the ball only a few times. Passing is the most complicated thing in football. A lot can go wrong, and interceptions occur often at youth levels. Turnovers are a heavy price and coaches worry about putting the ball up too much. I believe much of the problem comes from lack of proper form with the

Figure 16
TACKLE

Focus on the belt.

Feet balanced, drive into opponent and wrap.

Get shoulder into the runner.

Take what you can get.

Figure 17
TAKE SNAP SECURELY

The quarterback gets up to the center snugly and makes sure of a secure snap.

Hand position to receive the snap.

quarterback. They are nervous, excited, and inexperienced, and the first thing that goes under pressure is form. I doubt that youth coaches emphasize it enough. It seems that they rely too much on the natural ability of their passer.

However, there are some essentials of passing form that create a solid foundation for a young quarterback, and that can greatly add to passing accuracy. Let's discuss them. If you practice them with your son there will soon be a noticeable difference in his poise, confidence, and success. The mechanics of passing are not difficult, but they must be practiced with enough repetition so that they become automatic. From such a foundation of strength and stability the player can perform at a higher level.

We'll discuss pass patterns in Chapter 5.

Snap and Retreat

1) Think! A pass play begins as soon as the quarterback breaks the huddle. He sizes up the defense. His gaze must be impassive, always starting from the same side of the field and slowly sweeping and scanning the secondary. Can he spot a blitz? Is a defender out of position? Where are the seams? Where will there be a height mismatch? Has the wind changed and does it favor a long or short pass? How do things "feel"?

2) Take the snap comfortably. The hands should be firmly pressed against the center's crotch; firmly enough so that the center clearly knows exactly where they are. The passing hand is on top, other hand on the bottom. The insides of the wrists are touching with the fingers spread (some rotate the hand a bit so that the thumbs are up more—do what's comfortable!). The key is to take the snap securely and quickly. (See Figure 17.)

3) Retreat quickly. A right-handed player will quickly turn to the right, push off with the left foot, and step back with the right foot. Sometimes he will fake a hand-off to slow down the defensive charge. Some quarterbacks will simply back-pedal the entire 4-6 yards. Although this provides a clearer view of the secondary, there is a chance of tripping. Whatever method is used, the idea is to get back very quickly so that there is time to pick up the downfield action. The snap, the footwork, the pivot, the quick drop-back, and the number of steps taken should be practiced repeatedly. Keep the hands high at the end of the retreat. Quick-outs (passes to the flat) or quick slant passes may require only one to three steps.

Most other passes require five steps, always starting and ending with the right (back) foot (if the quarterback is right-handed). Practice these steps. Make them routine. Fumbles or missteps occur often, and they can turn a whole game around. Make it all automatic, so that in a game situation the passer can focus more on his primary receiver and on the reaction of the defensive secondary.

4) Step forward. Once the passer takes the prescribed number of steps backward, he should stop, pause, and then take a step forward. The outside pass rusher will angle on the back point of his drop, and so the final step forward into the "pocket" will afford more protection. Of course, if there is a weakness up the middle, and pressure comes from there, adjustments must be made. The quarterback may need to *roll out* to the flat to buy more time. The object is to stay cool, don't panic, and focus downfield. Get the pass off, not recklessly or in desperation, but under control. If a sack occurs it is always better than an interception.

5) Grip the ball, hands up at the shoulder. In the normal retreat the quarterback should hold the ball up even with the shoulder by the side of his head, using a proper passing grip in the throwing hand and protecting the ball with the other hand. The left or free hand should be kept on the ball, protecting it until ready to release it. This is a good habit; develop it early and it will definitely save an occasional fumble. The ball should be gripped snugly, not squeezed, with the fingers spread wide and touching the ball along their entire length. The hand grips it in back of center, with the pinky near the middle of the ball. The laces are under the last joints of the fingers. Some space should exist between the side of the palm and the ball. Again, comfort is desirable. A wide finger spread is the best, but, of course, large hands are needed for that. Special exercises to stretch the fingers backward and sideways can improve the grip and should be done. (See Figure 18.)

The Pass Release

1) Survey, stand erect, hold the ball high, and step to the receiver. Okay, now for the moment of truth. The first job is to decide who gets the ball. Usually, that's already planned by the play pattern called in the huddle. The pattern will send two or three receivers into the defensive secondary and is designed so that the *primary* receiver will wind up with only individual coverage, one-on-one. Even the timing of the throw is sometimes pre-determined

Figure 18
GRIP

Retreat with the ball high, protect it with the free hand, and look at developing pass patterns.

Grip back of center, laces under tip joints of fingers.

Figure 19
WRIST SNAP

Survey, stand erect with the ball high, and take a small step toward the receiver.

Snap wrist for spiral, roll ball off fingertips.

so that the passer knows about when the receiver will break to one side, or speed up and go deep. The idea usually is to hit the receiver just after he breaks to one side, since that is when the defender will be farthest from him, particularly if the receiver has faked convincingly to the other side.

Passers usually try to hit a receiver as he moves from one defensive zone to another, since he is most "open" when he is *in the seam* between defenders. However, the passer needs to be flexible to know how far the defender is from his primary receiver, to see if another defender is double-teaming his primary, and perhaps then to take a peek at his secondary receiver. For all of this, the passer has only a second or two. He must stand erect to get the fullest possible vision, legs comfortable but not spread apart too much. His weight is on the back—usually the right—foot. The quarterback holds the ball high and then steps toward his target, toward where the receiver should be when the ball arrives. *Make sure not to take too big a step since that will cause a late release and an underthrown pass.* A half a yard is fine—just a moderate step! (See Figure 19.)

2) Snap the wrist. On a long pass, we want the nose of the ball tilted up a bit so that it floats and settles safely into the receiver's hands. Of course, the farther the pass, the more the passer needs to lead the receiver. If there is to be a mistake on a long pass, it is better to err by overthrowing. The arm must move straight as the weight is shifted to the front foot. The free arm is extended, preferably in the direction of the pass. The forward arm movement is very quick and *snaps the wrist* in a whipping motion, rolling the ball off the fingers, little finger first. The wrist snap is what causes the ball to spiral evenly, and a nice spiral is easier to catch. The wrist brings the hand and fingers downward and inward as the ball rolls away. The spin need not, and should not, be too fast—just moderate.

A short pass needs an even harder wrist snap. It must be fired very hard since the ball must quickly thread its way through several outreaching defensive hands. It's usually better to underthrow a short pass if an error is to be made, since there usually are more defenders deep. Hold the nose of the ball level or even down a hair. In any case, follow through fully.

3) Jump passes. Often passes have to be thrown while the quarterback is on the run. Initially the ball is held to the side to hide it. Then, raise and hold the ball high, faking the release if possible to slow a charging defender or perhaps get him to jump. If the secondary drops back, a run may be possible. Otherwise throw, but remember that less of a *lead* is needed if the receiver is moving in the same direction (to compensate for the passer's own momentum). If the passer must jump to get more strength on the pass or to avoid a defender, he should release the ball with a quick wrist snap at the top of the jump. It's useful to take the final step a bit forward, if possible, to get some momentum on the ball.

Drills

The ideal pass is about 10-15 yards long, so these should be practiced the most. Rest the arm on consecutive days. Remember that your son is throwing in practice, so your assistance is best during the off-season, or during times when he has not been throwing too much. Have him throw to you; it's a good workout. Do about twenty to thirty passes, going in and out, across the middle, quick short passes. Don't wear out his arm with too many long bombs, and save them for the end when he has loosened up plenty.

Have him practice with a wet ball. It will rain sometimes, and experience with a wet ball is very useful on such days. Sometimes it's necessary on short passes to face the palm out more to maintain grip and contact on a wet ball. Let him attempt different approaches to find what works best. He should also pass off-balance in practice. I don't know why coaches don't practice it, but it will happen in a game and that is what practice is for—to help execute better under game conditions. The hardest pass is when fading backward (and probably should not be thrown), but practice it anyway. One parent can rush him, and he can throw to someone else.

RECEIVING

Nothing gets a crowd going like a long, beautiful pass reception. Receivers, especially wide receivers, have become a rare breed of their own. They are agile athletes, preferably tall, are great leapers, have super quick speed, and are players with enormous courage. No one gets hit as hard as a receiver coming down with his full weight into a helmet or shoulder of a tough defender.

It takes a few years before you will see many passes at youth levels. Coaches know that the 50% completion rate in the pro's is many times higher than that for nine- to thirteen-year-old kids. Interceptions are common at young ages. Again, this is an area where kids don't get a lot of work. Unfortunately, in most states, as with many youth sports, there are limits to the amount of practice kids get. In my hometown, the kids practice only twice a week during the season. In some leagues there is a limit to the number of practice hours allowed. Also, there are often no lights for evening practice, although more and more towns now have lights.

There are some definite guidelines for receivers to follow.

1) Get off the line. I haven't seen many youth teams that check or delay the offensive end or wide receiver at the line of scrimmage. The idea is to delay the receiver so the passer has less time to pass. It is more common in high school, perhaps because more passes are thrown at older ages. In any event, if someone tries to delay your son he must know that a quick fake step to one side, with arms out front, and perhaps a "shiver and shed" move will be needed. Sometimes, just a blast of speed around the defender is sufficient.

2) Run directly at the defender. This is a crucial first move. The natural impulse is to angle away from the defender, but that removes the ability to fake. Run hard right at the defender, as fast as possible, as if to run right through him. This will take away any chance he has to anticipate the receiver's ultimate direction, and it should help to get him a bit off-balance.

3) Make the move just as the defender commits. Once he starts retreating, *fully committed and back-pedaling sufficiently*, then put on the next move. This means the receiver needs to concentrate on the defender's momentum. If he is back-pedaling quickly, a fake may not be needed; just cut quickly and sharply according to the pass pattern. However, a fake can usually help, *so take two or three steps to one direction and then cut sharply to the other*. A head fake or a one-step fake is often not enough. The second or third step will change the defender's momentum and spring the receiver loose for the pass. Move quickly, but under control, particularly in the final steps of the pattern. There is no need for full speed; save a bit to allow for a reaction to the pass—it may be short or long.

4) Don't forget your quarterback. The passer is under tremendous pressure and may need to unload early. How often does a pass fall near a receiver who never turned to see what was happening? The receiver must look to the passer as soon as he breaks from his fake. Forget the defender the passer needs some attention now —don't make him wait. Make eye contact as quickly as possible.

5) Focus, soft hands, wait for the ball. When the ball is up in

Figure 20
RECEIVING

Make the cut sharply (as done here by #23) and quickly look toward the passer.

Touchdown! How sweet it is. The ball was caught while the receiver was airborne.

Figure 21
THE RUNNING BACK

The glory of football is decidedly still found in the breakaway running play.

the air, quick decisions have to be made. Speed is adjusted to meet the ball. *Eyes must be on the ball.* Don't reach for it until it gets close; if you do you can tip off the defender as to its timing. Often the defender will turn his back on the ball and use the receiver's body language to signal when it's time to turn for the ball. So don't reach early, and try to remain calm. The arms and hands should be relaxed, with soft fingers ready to receive the ball. Gently withdraw the hands upon contact to soften the impact.

   6) Catch it high, use the hands, fingers curled and spread. A pass should be caught *as high as possible.* First, this reduces the chance for an interception. Second, it gets the receiver off the ground. The body is smooth as it glides through the air, but it is bumpy while running; getting off the feet helps for a smooth catch. Also, catch with the hands and curl the fingers. The fingers should curl into the form of the ball. If they are straight, the ball will tend to bounce off the palm. Too often kids try to trap the ball with the arms. It's okay to use the chest and arms to trap the ball, but the hands are always more effective. (See Figure 20.)

   Here's a really helpful hint! *Focus on the front tip of the ball and try to catch it.* Try this yourself and tell your son to try it. It really helps to focus concentration and hand placement. *Watch the ball all the way into the hands.* This is critical. A useful practice drill is to watch the spin of the ball or try to see the laces spinning as you catch it. A receiver has a certain "oneness" with the ball. He feels as though he has already caught it while it is still in the air—it's his!

   In a deep pattern the receiver arches his back and raises his hands, palms back. On a "button hook" he faces the ball, hands in a "W" shape. On a pass across the middle the best place to catch the ball is just in front of the inside shoulder. Catch and tuck it in before running. This may sound obvious, but kids often think about running before they secure the catch, or maybe they are bracing for an expected hit. The primary and over-all most important job for a receiver is to firmly catch and tuck the ball before doing anything else.

   7) Change direction immediately. The defense will tend to flow with the receiver's momentum and direction, so it is usually quite effective to make an immediate change of direction after a reception. The move is particularly recommended when the receiver does not know where the coverage is around him. This will help to break away for a few more yards, or perhaps will spring a long run. A spin move also helps at this point. However, remember that the most important thing is to have the ball tucked in securely.

8) Recover and tackle if intercepted. If this happens, chances are you have the best first shot at the tackle. Recover immediately. Don't get mad at yourself; don't turn into a spectator. Go get the opponent and bring him down.

Drills

As with passing, the best drill is just doing it. If your son is young you may wish to throw while down on one knee to simulate the height of the normal ball release of his quarterback. If there are a few kids around, set them up in a secondary and keep throwing. Have your checklist handy and keep calling out these helpful hints. It's good for him to practice catching passes with one hand. Throw to one side, then to the other. It helps to train the hands to react properly.

RUNNING

At the grade school level, football is a running game. The great majority of plays involve running the ball, and most yardage seems to be gained on wide running sweeps. Often the team with a real speedster will break open big plays around the end for the score. Of course, plays are also run up the middle, but blocking techniques are usually not very well developed yet, and so defensive linemen and linebackers pretty much control the middle. (See Figure 21.)

Most people seem to feel that the glory of football is found at the running back position. I guess over the years the Jim Browns, the Walter Paytons, and the O.J. Simpsons have gotten the most exposure. Anyone who has played football has great respect for all positions, and knows that the fierce hand-to-hand combat in the middle of the line is really the heart and soul of the game. However, the running backs put the numbers up on the scoreboard. They get hit very hard and earn every bit of their attention. My son played fullback his first year, and while he didn't have great speed, he used to buck the line with a full and reckless abandon, dropping his shoulder and often giving a linebacker a shot of his own.

Let's Talk Basics

1) **The stance.** The runner needs to have a stance from which

he can move in any direction with ease and quickness. As with the linemen, they start with a "ready" position—feet spread apart, hands on the knees, and eyes straight ahead. Then they drop into a set position. Some coaches prefer them to stay up in ready position since this allows for a better read of the developing hole they must run through, but it sacrifices quickness. I much prefer the set position.

In the set position the legs are fairly wide apart, outside of the shoulders. The extra width helps lateral movement, and most running plays, except for dives straight up the middle, require lateral movement. *It is important to be able to move laterally very quickly,* so a spread and balanced foot position allows for a push to either side. One foot, usually the inside foot, is set back, but only a few inches behind the front. Again, this helps balance. The hand on the side as the back foot is straight down, but not much weight is on it. It is mainly for balance. The head is up and the back straight like a lineman. The body is tense, coiled, and ready to spring. The toes are straight ahead, or even pointed outward a bit since the push comes from the inside-front or *balls* of the feet. (See Figure 22.)

It is essential to get into the exact same stance every play. Don't lean! *Don't look to the side where the play will go!* Head, shoulders, and eyes are forward and impassive. The defense is looking intently for a clue as to where the play will go. Don't help them out.

2) **Pivot and snap.** As I watch pre-high school games, I am struck by how long it takes for the backfield action to develop. Often, I hear parents screaming for kids to "Block, Block, Block better," but the real problem is often that the running back gets to the hole too late. A blocker gives a jolt, as stated earlier, and attempts to sustain the block, but the defender can use his hands freely to shed him. Therefore, the running back must get there before the defender fully recovers. A split second makes all the difference in the world, especially at young ages when sustained blocking is the exception and not the rule. The four or five yards between the running back and the line of scrimmage are critical. Getting there quickly is more important than what happens later. In fact, the first move, the pivot and snap, is the most important of all.

Running backs must fully pivot towards their intended direction before they ever take a step. They snap the head and shoulders in that direction, shifting weight by pushing off the ball of the foot opposite to that direction. Only *after* the pivot do they take the first, large step, with the foot closest to the intended direction.

Figure 22
RUNNING BACK STANCE

The two deep backs have legs spread ready to move laterally, with little weight forward. The fullback, however, has a lot of weight forward since he is going straight ahead (and perhaps tipping it off!).

Figure 23
PIVOT AND SNAP

Notice how these backs pivot and snap to the right before they take a step.

Stepping first just wastes time. It is much quicker to pivot first and then step out directly. This technique must be practiced until it is automatic. The head and shoulder snap adds to the overall quickness of the move. Take off low, stay low, and then build up speed with strong churning arm movement. (See Figure 23.)

3) **Look at the hole; receive the hand-off securely.** Don't worry about the quarterback. It is his job to get the ball to the runner safely. The runner must look at the gap he will run through. He scrutinizes the area to see what is developing and to see whether a key block will be successful.

The quarterback should present the ball firmly, usually with one hand on the outside and underside of the ball, well into the runner's midsection, just above the belt. The quarterback *must focus squarely on the runner's belt*. If the play is into the middle of the line, the runner will receive it with the far arm relaxed down in front of the opposite hip, palm toward the ball, and the elbow and forearm nearest the quarterback raised chest high, ready to help cover and secure the ball. He then curls both hands around the opposite tips of the ball. Cover the tips — don't just circle them. On a wide play the runner may receive it in the midsection, or he may take it with the hands, depending on the speed and motion needed.

4) **Carry the ball securely.** Most fumbles do not occur because of a powerful defensive jolt, but because the ball was not carried securely. In one game my son's team, a very strong team, lost the ball on the first play of their first two possessions because the same running back carried the ball through the line like it was a flag, waving it around wildly. It was the only game we lost that season.

The proper technique is to jam the point of the ball into the pocket between the upper arm and ribs, just below the armpit. The forearm is stretched along the side of the ball, slightly to the underside. The upper hand is curled around the front tip, fingers spread to the inside. The technique is designed to protect the ball, and every protection is needed. The tackler will not only hit hard, he is instructed to try to tear or slash the ball free, especially the second tackler on the scene. (See Figure 24.)

The ball is carried in the right arm when running right and in the left arm when running left. When running in the open field, the runner may switch hands to get the ball away from the nearest approaching tackler, but only if he is absolutely sure there is time. Make sure the new hand has the ball before sliding it across the

Figure 24
SECURE THE BALL

Secure the ball snug in the armpit.

This ball is just looking to be fumbled.

Figure 25
RUN HARD

Stay balanced and keep charging forward as long as possible.

Run through the tackler for extra yardage.

midsection for the switch.

5) **Run with power, run hard, and give a second effort.** Now it's time to get yardage. The single focus of the running back must be to get as much yardage as possible. Don't worry about the tackler; look mainly for daylight. When a tackler appears, continue to run hard—get that precious yardage. Avoid his shoulder, run right through his arms, twist, turn, and keep the legs underneath with short driving steps. Fall forward or lunge for the extra few inches. One of the truly beautiful phrases in football is *second effort*. With this concept in mind and with determination to fight through contact he will gain much more yardage. (See Figure 25.)

6) **Straight-arm and other maneuvers.** I don't see the *straight-arm* too much anymore, yet it is a most useful weapon against the tackle. This idea is to reach out just as the tackler lunges. Place the palm out onto his shoulder or helmet. Point the shoulder at him and firmly straighten out and lock the arm. Don't give the arm too early or he will avoid (or grab) it. As soon as the arm makes contact, leap a bit. It will substantially reduce the tackler's jolt, and can catapult the runner a few yards. A stiff arm can also be effective to push the tackler down or away, particularly if he is off-balance.

Another move is the *step-out*, by which the runner jabs a sharp step towards the tackler to get him to tense up and then, perhaps with a straight-arm, pushes off laterally away from him. The runner can also pivot from a jab step by merely swinging the other foot around in a full 360 degree turn away from the defender's momentum. The *crossover* is a third avoidance measure in which the leg nearest the tackler is lifted high and away as the body also leans away. This is usually effective on a sweep or wide play before the defender gets too close.

However, most often the runner will buck the line on a dive or off-tackle run, keeping the body low, both arms protecting the ball, short steps, turning, rolling, head up, eyes open, looking for just one more inch.

SPECIALTIES

We'll discuss special teams more a bit later when we review the overall strategy of offense and defense. Special teams are used for kicking, primarily for kickoffs, field goals, points after the touchdown, and punts. As you can see, these teams are on the field mainly when possession is being formally transferred to the opponent (kickoff and punt) or when attempting to score by place-kicking (field goal and point after touchdown). They are the wild and woolly times of football since the action is often spread over the entire field, players are running at full speed, and anything can happen. There are a few very special and quite important skills involved, particularly kicking skills, and your child may want to seriously consider developing them. From nine to thirteen years old the kicks in the kickoff normally range from 20-40 yards, increasing about 4-5 yards each year. More often than not the ball is miskicked and travels close to the ground, bouncing after 15 yards. Try your son at punting and place-kicking, particularly if he has played soccer. Good kickers are *very rare and very valuable* to grade school teams, and with a bit of practice it is incredible how quickly he can improve. Most kids just never try it. Other specialties such as catching punts and kickoffs and hiking the snaps for kickers are also important. We'll discuss each of them.

At the very young ages punting is often avoided unless *very* long yardage is needed for a first down, or the team is backed up very near their own goal line. The potential for disaster is quite high. A bad snap, poor blocking, a slow punter all combine to discourage coaches from trying it, particularly when the successful kick often gains only 10-15 yards, as often is the case. Coaches figure the heck with it. They take their chances with a sweep around the end and hope to get lucky.

The Snap

In the pro's, the punter lines up 12-15 yards behind the line of scrimmage. At youth levels it is 7-10 yards, and that's still quite a hike for a young center. The field goal or point after touchdown (P.A.T.) snap is a few yards shorter, although place-kicks are still quite rare at the youth level. The snap should be practiced regularly by the center, preferably with the team's actual punter or place-kick holder. It is similar to an upside down pass; the harder and faster the better. A fast snap can save a precious split second and avoid a blocked punt.

The center should get into a normal stance, with the back foot a bit farther back if that is more comfortable. Raise the front point of the ball. Place the right hand up near the front similar to a passer's grip, with the left hand on the side of the ball to help guide it, particularly if the hands are small. The left hand leaves the ball first. Weight is moderately forward upon the ball, as is normal for snaps. Drive the ball back in a quick snapping motion, aiming for the area between the knee and the waist of the punter, or directly to the hands of the place-kick holder. Give the ball as little arc as possible and make the snap hard. Make sure that the snap is completed before worrying about the nose guard; the snap is more important than he is. Blocked punts are always a major disaster. Brace and step forward *with the snap* for balance.

Punting

The punter looks only at the ball, nothing else. His feet are parallel. The weight is on the left foot if he is a righty. The arms are extended outward, palms down and inward, thumbs up, and fingers spread and curled a bit. He stands erect, hands soft, body relaxed. Now concentrate and let the ball come all the way to the hands. The hands should withdraw slightly to soften contact. Place the laces up, right hand back a bit, cradling the ball. Take a short step with the kicking foot and a second longer and quicker step with the plant foot, planting it firmly and securely. Survey the plant area beforehand to ensure that there is good footing. Extend and serve the ball over the kicking leg, the front pointed downward a little and turned slightly to the inside. Place the ball on the foot with the right hand. Don't "drop" it too far; the less distance it travels the better.

The kick will spiral if the ball is kicked with the outside of the instep, with the right side of the shoe laces contacting the underbelly of the ball. It will travel end over end if kicked on the instep squarely along the bottom seam of the ball. The knee at first is relaxed. As it comes forward, it whips the rigidly locked ankle forward in a hard snapping motion. This is what gives power and distance to the punt. The foot comes forward in a smooth pendulum motion, not sideways, and follows through to shoulder height at least, pulling the body forward in a hopping motion. The left arm may raise up and swing across the chest to help balance and torque. The punter only has a couple of seconds to do all of this. He must be quick, balanced, under control, and cool. Good practice drills have the punter kick about 5-10 yards, to a teammate (or to a parent) slowly, watching the form and point of contact with

Figure 26
PUNT

Punts are often avoided at youth levels. Practice here can make your son a rare and valuable asset.

Receive punts with the hands and then bring into the body.

Figure 27
PLACEKICKING

This specialty takes years to develop, but can win an important position for a determined player.

the ball, trying to lay the ball on the instep with as little extra distance as possible. Have him tap it to you, and he should learn enough control so you don't have to move to catch it at all. Then, overcompensate the other way, booming kicks for maximum power and distance. Try to get the kick away in about two seconds from the snap. (See Figure 26.)

Catching Punts

The receiver stands about 5 yards deeper than the punter can kick so that he is moving forward as he receives the ball. This could add at least 5 yards to the return. The receiver should have his arms raised forward and upward a bit. Palms should be up, fingers spread, and hands fairly close together. The ball should always be caught with the hands and then brought into the midsection quickly for protection. The body and hands should withdraw, even squat a bit, to soften impact.

Place-Kicking

Soccer-style kicking has pretty much taken over football. It gives just as much power and much more accuracy than the toe kicking of olden days. If your son has a good strong foot, try him at it. The kicker takes two or three steps, depending on the distance needed, in a quarter-circle motion. He measures the distance and stands with legs even, leaning forward a bit on the front foot. The holder kneels on the left knee near where he will place the ball, right leg extended forward, arms reaching towards the ball. He receives the snap, lowers the ball to the spot, turns the laces facing forward (out of the way of the foot), and places the end of the right hand exactly on the tip, removing the left hand. He always looks only at the ball. It should be nearly straight up, tilted a hair backwards, depending on the kicker's preference. The kicker takes the two or three steps and plants the free foot pointing straight at the target, toes even with the back of the ball and several inches to the side, depending on the kicker's comfort and style. (See Figure 27.)

The kickoff is just a long place-kick, except that the kicker takes numerous steps, covering at least 5 yards. The ball is kicked off a tee. Otherwise, the techniques are the same. Kids can kickoff at a range of 20-40 yards. If your son can consistently deliver 30 plus yards by age ten, he should try out for this position.

3.
FIELD POSITIONS

WHAT POSITION SHOULD YOUR SON PLAY?

Well, that's mainly up to the coach. During the first practice or two he will usually ask kids to split up into positions of their own choice, but very quickly the coach will determine where they play. The first wind sprints, 30-40 yard dashes, will tell the coach where his speed is, and speed is the primary determinant separating backs and linemen. Usually, the coach will have several rules of thumb; sometimes he must assign a person to a certain position just because there is no one else on the team who can play that position. Remember, and remind your son, *it is a team sport*, and he must play where he is needed most.

In general, the fastest kids play in the *backfield* on both offense and defense. The biggest, more heavily built kids play on the *line*. Aggressive kids who combine speed, strength, and agility play *linebacker*. Taller kids who have some quickness play *end*; offensive end if they can catch and block, defensive end if they can make tackles. In fact, if any kid has aggressiveness and can produce tackles, the coach will find him a place somewhere on *defense*. Big, strong, but slower kids play *offensive line*, and the largest kids in this group play tackle. (See Figure 28.)

The quarterback is the one who has it all: brains to spare, a

Figure 28
FIELD POSITIONS

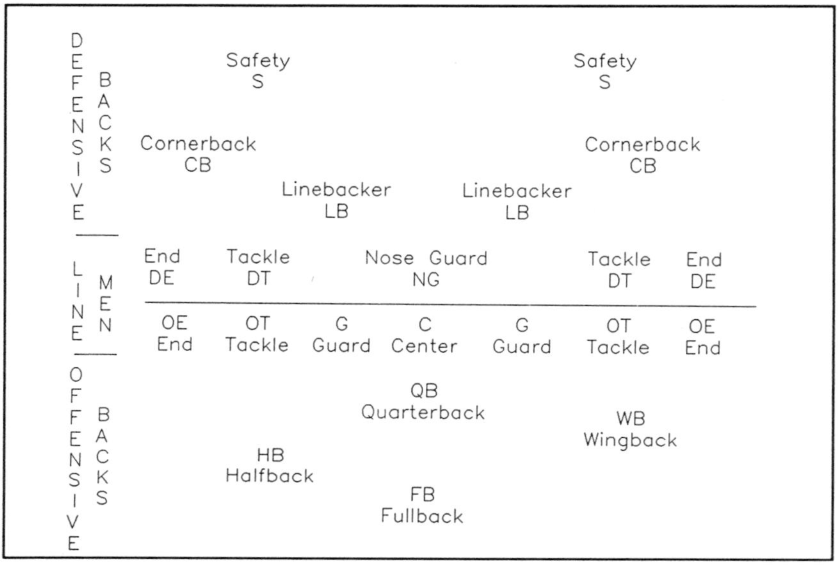

```
D
E
F          Safety                        Safety
E   B        S                             S
N   A
S   C
I   K   Cornerback                    Cornerback
V   S      CB                             CB
E            Linebacker      Linebacker
                 LB              LB

L       End   Tackle   Nose Guard    Tackle   End
I   M   DE     DT          NG          DT      DE
N   E
E   N   OE    OT    G     C     G     OT     OE
        End  Tackle Guard Center Guard Tackle End

O                         QB
F                      Quarterback
F   B                                  WB
E   A                                Wingback
N   C        HB
S   K     Halfback
I   S                   FB
V                     Fullback
E
```

strong arm, and the ability to complete passes. He must be able to
receive snaps, remember complex plays (not just his role, but everyone else's too), and hand off the ball securely.

Sure, coaches will have favorites. Sometimes it does not seem
fair who gets to play where. But a coach's main motivation is to
succeed, and he will generally put kids where they fit best. *A kid's
attitude plays a large role too!* If a coach has a close call, he will give
a prime position to a nicer kid. The kid who has a bad attitude, who
is over-sensitive, or who demonstrates any sort of problem will be
passed over. This goes for the allocation of playing time also. A
negative attitude will cost your son, so make sure he knows this.

I believe that football is generally good for a kid with a bad attitude. Most sports quickly teach a kid the price they pay for acting
up, so they have a chance to deal with it. They want to play so they
try to change. Hopefully, they get a coach who helps them control
their emotions, instead of one who makes it worse. I've seen coaches
get pretty nasty with a kid who needs a friend, and even drive the
kid away from the game.

At some point, your son may come home upset because his visions of scoring touchdowns have been dashed by an assignment to another position. I touched on this earlier but it bears repeating. He'll get over it! Don't exacerbate his frustration. He will learn how to have just as much fun tackling ball-carriers or opening holes for them. Remind him that the coach has to go with the faster guy in the backfield; that it's a team sport; and that he should just try to be as good as he can be at the assigned position.

In the backfield, the biggest and strongest of the running backs is usually the fullback. He needs to be strong to run up the middle into heavy traffic. The fastest, most elusive kid is a halfback, wingback, or flanker and usually runs wide sweeping plays around the whole pack.

On the line, the biggest kids are tackles—the pillars of the line. Quicker linemen are guards since they move around a lot, pulling, trapping, and leading running backs. A stable, courageous, strong-legged kid who can securely snap the ball as he is about to get creamed will play center. He is the most important of the linemen since he guards the most valuable turf on the field.

That's a thumbnail sketch of positions. There is a position on the field for your child. Coaches will vary as to their views. Let's talk a bit more about each specific position. Please keep in mind that the general basic skills were covered in detail in Chapter 2 and won't be discussed here in any depth. The idea here is to focus more on the nature of each position, and what the player will need to understand about it.

OFFENSIVE POSITIONS

Center

The center is just that—he plays the center of the line. His role is to snap the ball to the quarterback, avoid a fumble, and still make a good block on his man. He has to have perfect timing synchronized to the quarterback's cadence, or his hike will be late and his team will be offside.

The center has a slightly different stance from the rest of the line. His feet are spread wide and his hips must be high to allow for easy passage of the ball between his legs. The legs are positioned fairly evenly so as not to trip the quarterback. The weight is moderately forward on the ball. Kids often need two hands on the snap,

Figure 29
THE CENTER

Center (see arrow) is a tough job, and it takes a special kid to play center. Note that the other offensive linemen are lined up too far back.

Figure 30
THE GUARD

This player (see arrow) must be quick and scrappy. He usually goes after linebackers or pulls to trap defensive linemen. He also pulls to lead runners through a hole.

Figure 31
THE TACKLE

The pillars of the line. Tacklers are called upon to move the defensive tacklers out of the way.

although one hand is better, freeing up the other to deal with the opponent. The center's head may be in, but not beyond the neutral zone between the front and rear of the ball. The head is over, but not past, the end of the ball. The arm is extended and he turns and tilts the ball as is needed for a good snap. Head is up. (See Figure 29.)

The center must snap quickly at the precise time. A very quick, firm snap is essential. The elbow bends slightly and he releases the ball to the quarterback. Of course, the snap is practiced thousands of times. Usually the quarterback wants the ball on a certain angle to fit his hand, with the laces hitting the hand by the fingertips. Different quarterbacks do it differently—this is why fumbles occur often in a game when quarterbacks are switched. The correct angle and degree of the snap must be worked out. The center's hand also needs to be well forward on the top of the ball so that it is opposite the quarterback's hands upon transfer.

The center may step forward *as he snaps*. It may be a simultaneous motion, stepping and snapping. This is true only for the center; other linemen can't begin to move forward until the ball is already in motion. The center's first step must be very quick and should be straight forward, not to the side. He angles his head to the runner's side and *gives a quick pop* to the opponent. He should step with the foot closest to the side where the play will go.

See Chapter 2 for snapping on punts and kicks.

Guards

On each side of the center are the guards. Offensive linemen all need strong legs since their principal job is to drive opponents away from their positions. However, guards also need to be quick. The guard often pulls out along the line of scrimmage to trap an opponent charging across the line, hitting him from the side. Guards also lead the runner through a hole. We discussed *pulling skills* earlier; the idea basically is to take a short step and push off with the down hand and with the foot opposite the direction of the pull. Bend the knees, stay close to scrimmage, and jolt the opponent good. (See Figure 30.)

Guards very often block the defensive end on wide running plays. I played defensive end in high school and my most enduring memories are of guards charging towards me, pumping their arms for strength, eyes wide open upon my midsection, coming in fast and low. I was tall, so I could never get under them. I just had to use my arm strength to shiver them and keep them away long enough to find the ball-carrier. I certainly didn't always succeed.

Guards need to use their entire body more than other linemen. Cross body blocks, crab blocks (see Chapter 2 on blocks), whatever they can do to interfere with their opponent. Guards often get to trap the nose guard. However, the toughest defender on the field is usually the linebacker, and guards most often draw him. They must use their quickness against an equally quick opponent, and somehow stay between him and the ball-carrier. Blocking linebackers is clearly the toughest job for the offensive guard.

Tackles

Next to the guards are the tackles. I played this position on offense for a few years. Tackles are usually the biggest linemen. They generally block straight forward into a defensive tackle who is just as big as they are. Sometimes they block a linebacker or an end, or they go downfield to block a defensive back if the play goes to the opposite side of the field. They rarely pull, although it does occur occasionally. Size and strength are needed since this position involves pretty much a *one-on-one, straight ahead, short distance power struggle* between two big players. (See Figure 31.)

Offensive running plays, as will be discussed later, usually are dives up the middle, slants off-tackle (that is, outside of the tackle between him and the end), or wide sweeps around the end. On dives up the middle, the tackle shoots forward a step and stays between his opponent and the ball. However, on wide plays the defender has the outside advantage and so the job is much tougher. On sweeps, the idea is to delay the opponent from penetrating. Off-tackle plays, however, require the best effort. The opponent must be driven out of the area and turned away. This is the toughest job for the tackle, although a cross block pattern will help.

Ends

The end needs to be tall and quick enough to catch short passes, but he must also be strong enough to block the defensive end and even the big defensive tackle when called to do so. In fact, the tight end spends most of his time blocking, and these skills must be worked on even more than receiving. The great tight ends like Mark Bavaro of the New York Giants are also great blockers. I played offensive end in my earliest years (before I got so big that I could block better than I could catch and was moved to tackle!). I truly loved this position since I got a chance to catch passes.

A very effective pass is a quick slant where the tight end dashes directly towards the middle, and the quarterback, who doesn't even drop back, fires the ball to him from close range. It's a tough pass to catch since it must be a hard-thrown one, but it's quite effective. Often a defender will try to jam the end—just give him a shot to slow him down—and of course this can eliminate the effectiveness of a quick slant pass.

A split end is an end who lines up at least several yards from the tackle and is primarily a pass catcher. The end's stance is similar to that of the other linemen. He is usually a yard or so outside of the offensive tackle.

Often, the end is called upon to block downfield. These are always difficult blocks since defensive backs are very quick and agile and can use their hands fully. Usually the best that can be hoped for is just to slow them down a step, *but that is also important*. Kids often don't regard downfield blocking as important, yet *a good downfield block, more than any other block, can spring a touchdown*. Remind your son that he must play until the whistle blows, and to keep blocking someone.

Wide Receiver

Split ends, wide receivers, and running backs all go out for the long passes. They line up very wide to try to ensure only one-on-one coverage. They need great speed, the quickness to fake a defender (see Chapter 2 on receiving), and the courage to concentrate on receiving a pass while about to be hit hard. At the pre-high school level, football is not a passing game since there are usually as many interceptions as completions. However, the wide receiver is still out there, waiting for his day to see the long pass sailing towards him against that blue sky. I think this is one of the truly great moments in all of football. Fans hold their breath. Things seem momentarily suspended; the ball is high in the air. No downfield contact is allowed while the ball is in flight, and the fleet-footed players are running at full throttle to snatch the ball from the air. Long pass receptions are clearly the most popular plays in the pro's, and they are the most beautiful to behold.

Figure 32
THE HALFBACK

The great thrill of football is open field running, and halfbacks get to do it often.

Figure 33
THE FULLBACK

On a short yardage situation, we usually ask the big fullback (see arrow) to drive low into the middle for the first down.

Figure 34
THE QUARTERBACK

The quarterback—#34 running a team huddle here—is the field general.

Halfbacks

These players are usually the fastest kids on the offense and they do most of the ball-carrying for that reason. They spend some time blocking for the other backs and can also go out for a pass, but their primary job is to advance the ball. They run off-tackle or wide, usually leaving the short yardage, straight forward dives for the bigger fullback. We covered the stance, the pivot, and running skills in Chapter 2. The quick snap of head and shoulder, the pivot into the direction of the play, and then—not until then—the step out are the keys to a good, quick start. It also is essential not to tip off the defenders by looking or leaning in the desired direction before the hike. Remember, the linebackers are *carefully scanning* your face and stance for any clue as to the play. (See Figure 32.)

Halfbacks must move with explosive quickness in an endeavor to outrun the field, especially on wide sweeps or end runs. The moment of decision occurs when a defender approaches. Do I cut back? Do I try to dance and spin around? Do I lower my shoulder and ram forward, happy to settle for a few extra yards? The cut back and the fancy steps could spring long yardage, but also can lose a yard. The running-hard approach is more conservative and will usually gain a few yards. The halfback needs to learn what he is most successful at doing. *Remember, a few yards are a very valuable piece of territory!* It can be the difference between a first down or losing possession. I generally like to see the kids run hard and get the few extra yards, but the real key is for a player to follow his instincts.

Fullbacks

As noted earlier, fullbacks are usually the biggest and strongest of the running backs. They are asked to run the ball up the middle, usually on a straight dive play to one side of the center. They are expected to pick up a couple of yards regularly in short yardage situations. They run low and hard, with their heads up. They are expected to hit the hole very hard. It may not be a big hole, and they must capitalize on any advantage their blockers give them. Fullbacks don't dance much; they run hard and low and need a lot of momentum. They rely on their momentum to push the tackler back so that the fullback can fall forward, gaining every extra inch possible. Short, quick steps and churning legs can propel a fullback as he falls for an extra yard or so. Usually both hands are pressed over the ball, holding it firmly to the stomach. (See Figure 33.)

Fullbacks do a lot of blocking. They will lead the halfbacks on sweeps, off-tackle runs, or even dives. They block for the quarterback on passing plays. They must take fake hand-offs and convincingly draw linebackers to them as they pretend they have the ball.

Quarterbacks

Last and certainly not least is the team leader, the quarterback. This player is a top athlete, is cool, has good vision and a strong arm, is able to handle the ball securely, is agile in traffic, and is able to pass accurately even if on the run. He must know what everyone does on every play, and therefore needs to be quite intelligent. He must be a natural leader, able to motivate the players and to control his own intensity. *He must take charge on the field* and gain the respect of his teammates. (See Figure 34.) His footwork must be precise. Fakes must be very convincing; good habits are necessary here. The hand-off must be secure and, of course, passes must be accurate. The quarterback must learn when to throw, when and how to throw the ball away, and when to take a sack. He needs to understand when to scramble to avoid a loss of yardage. Often they learn the hard way, but they learn. When a play breaks up, or someone misses an assignment, the quarterback must be able to react, improvise, and go with the flow of the play. Chapter 2 already covered the fundamental basics of passing and hand-offs.

The worst thing for a quarterback is to fumble constantly, and it happens frequently at the youth level. Fumbles are killers to an offense trying to move the ball downfield and are most painful when they result not from contact but just from bad ball handling. Repeated practice taking snaps is quite necessary. They must take the snap securely *before* they pull back. Premature pulling back from snaps, perhaps from a slightly late snap, causes many fumbles. There is no better way to take the steam out of a drive than to drop the snap. To prevent a dropped snap, the quarterback must get low, bend the knees, and get the hands under the center's crotch far enough to secure the snap. Develop good habits here! Sharp, quick moves are necessary so the backs can run the ball through the hole before it closes. I often hear parents screaming for blocking when in fact the hole was there but delay in the backfield was the real problem.

Figure 35
THE NOSE GUARD

The toughest position in football is the nose guard (see arrow).

By just falling to the ground the nose guard can jam up the middle and still be in position to help the tackle (see arrow).

The quarterback lives in the eye of a swirling, grunting, clawing hurricane. He must stay poised. He can't worry about whether someone else is doing his job, but must go about his job with calmness and precision. Jerky, panicky moves lead to fumbles or cause a quarterback to trip or collide with his own players. He must also keep the offense coordinated and stay within the twenty-five seconds allotted to get a new play going after each down. He must know his personnel and try to find out where the defense is mismatched and where it is weak. When all else fails, he should rely on his most consistent teammate.

DEFENSIVE POSITIONS

Nose Guard

This position, head on to the offensive center, takes a special kind of kid! Action comes from all sides, and it is the quickest action in football. The most valuable piece of turf in the game is usually the one the nose guard stands upon. The offense will often double-team or trap him to get that piece of ground. So the main objective of the nose guard is to *hold his ground*.

His stance is a bit more solid and balanced than his teammates on the line. Often the stance is a four-point stance to ensure a low, well-braced charge. The worst thing for a nose guard to do is to stand up too quickly because, especially if double-teamed, he will be easy to move away. His charge should include a good shoulder jolt. Then he must crawl and scrape his way forward, always low enough that he cannot be driven away. The nose guard can submarine—shoot or dive low into the gap and scramble back to his feet. Another good move is to dive over a low charging center. But, most often, he jolts, sheds, and scraps like all linemen, just a bit lower. Even if he is on hands and knees he is at least blocking the hole, slowing down the runner, and piling up bodies in the middle. (See Figure 35.)

When double-teamed, the nose guard hits one blocker with his shoulder and fights off the other with his hands, turning his body sideways to claw his way through the seam between two blockers. Remember this is not a wrestling match; the idea is to shed. *A major fault with defensive linemen is that they tend to focus too much on wrestling with their opponents.* As stated in Chapter 2, the

Figure 36
DEFENSIVE TACKLES AND ENDS

The pillar of the defensive line, as well as one of the strongest kids on the team, is the defensive tackle (see arrow).

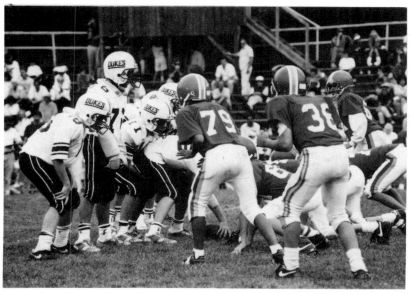

#79, the defensive end, is in good position—slight crouch, hands out, inside foot back.

idea is to hit the defender to neutralize his charge and to shed him quickly. Get rid of the blocker as fast as possible; don't play with him! It's not a contest to see who is stronger, but a contest to get away from the blocker.

Defensive Tackle

The foundation of the defense is at the tackle position. The nose guard is expected to ward off the runners and to stack up the middle ground; however, the tackle is expected to earn his name by tackling, tackling, tackling. Defensive tackles are usually the biggest and strongest kids on the team and are also aggressive enough to hold ground, penetrate, and bring the ball-carrier down. As with the nose guard, *they must hold their position*. They are responsible for tackling the ball-carrier on off-tackle plays. The main area they are responsible for is head on. The nose guard is often double-teamed, so the dive play up the middle must be looked for, although this play is the linebacker's main responsibility. At the least, tacklers must hold their ground, and if possible they should penetrate. On short yardage they hold and protect inside; on long yardage they penetrate, looking for a pass rush and a possible sack. They are always under control, prepared for the possible trap.

Usually, they line up on the outside shoulder of the offensive tackle on a five man line. The inside foot is back and it steps first, while the front foot drives inside toward the pressure. Remember, as noted above, defenders don't wrestle! Defensive tackles shed the blocker and drive a shoulder into the ball-carrier. They should avoid arm tackles since they are weak. However, if off-balance, tackles should grab whatever is available.

Most kids don't fully understand the effect of a good hard jolt upon their opponent. They use more of a shiver, hitting the blocker with their outstretched hands. Sometimes it looks just like they are playing patty-cake! A shiver move works for the end and the linebackers, but a down lineman is much better off to deal out a good shot and *then* to use the forearm and hands to shed and hunt. Keep saying to your son, "*Hit, shed, and hunt.*" (See Figure 36.)

Defensive End

Defensive end is a great position. I loved it when I played it. These kids are usually tall with good upper body strength to hold off blockers. Usually a defensive end has to ward off multiple blockers before he gets to the running back on an end run.

The defensive end is responsible for the outside, that is, for the wide running plays. He should penetrate for several steps, then turn and force the play to the inside where there is always more help and less running room. He is often blocked by a pulling guard, or by a fullback on an off-tackle play, and his job is to keep those plays to the inside, and even to force the action even farther inside. On a pass play the end is a key pass-rusher, and, like Lawrence Taylor of the New York Giants, he has a great angle to crash in on the quarterback.

The end stands up, arms at the side, crouched down a bit. He positions himself a bit outside the offensive end, or a yard or so off-tackle if the offensive end is split. The inside foot is back, and this foot steps forward first. He quickly penetrates a bit and then turns to face the play. We want the end to penetrate several yards, to guard against the sweep, but he is also looking to crash in on the off-tackle play or pursue a run to the other side. He must not be too quick to pursue, but look first for a possible reverse play before he leaves the area. The shiver charge described in Chapter 2 is usually the most effective weapon for the defensive end to use to ward off blockers.

The end, as is the case with all linemen, must be under control. He should not leave his feet if at all possible—particularly during a pass rush—since a faked pass can take him out of the action and thus open up the outside area to a scrambling quarterback. Philadelphia's Richard Cunningham is an expert at the fake pump and has left many a defensive end up in the air and out of control. The biggest mistake that ends make is getting faked inside, believing that it's an inside run. I remember it happening to me, and I remember the terrible feeling as I watched the real ball-carrier sweep untouched around my end on his way to big yardage. The end must hold the outside under all circumstances.

Linebacker

These are usually the toughest kids on the field. They are the heart of the defense. Their job is to figure out where the ball is going and to stop it. While a defensive lineman is expected to get blocked, perhaps double-teamed, and does not have the element of surprise, a linebacker has fewer excuses. He stands freely, with a

Figure 37
LINEBACKERS

The three linebackers behind the defensive line are the key to the defense.

few yards of space to react to the action. He must have a lot of upper body strength to throw off blockers, the agility to avoid them in the first instance, and a pounding aggressiveness.

Linebackers line up in a standing stance, leaning forward on the front of the feet, hands down and palms out, crouched and balanced, a yard or so behind the line of scrimmage. (See Figure 37.) Unless he is stunting, he is to scan the offense for clues as to where the play will go. Usually the offensive guards are the best clues, since on the snap they often move in the same direction as the ball. We will review the "keys" to reading offensive motion in Chapter 5. The linebacker must meet an approaching blocker with great strength and vigor, driving his forearm or straight arm into the blocker's upper body to neutralize him, and then quickly shedding him. He must directly address the head-on blocker, give a blow, shed, side step, and hunt the ball-carrier. The inside linebacker usually goes directly to the hole.

During a pass play, the outside linebacker angles to and looks to the flat on his side to pick up any receiver heading there and

Figure 38
DEFENSIVE SECONDARY

The last line of defense. They must pursue the tacklers and run a great deal.

Getting beat deep! The receiver, #22, has beaten the safety and a good throw here could score.

then prepares to cover that receiver. While outside linebackers have responsibility for the flat, inside linebackers mainly are concerned with defending against the short pass over the middle or a quarterback scramble.

Defensive Backs

The deep backs, safeties, and cornerbacks are fast, tough kids and are the last line of defense. They must come up and tackle anyone who gets past the defensive linemen and linebackers. Most important, they must catch the breakaway runner and prevent a score. They must be in great shape and have good endurance, because in this position they will run a lot. They head into downfield pursuit whenever the ball goes to the opposite side. *The biggest mistake they can make is to fail to get into pursuit to cut off a breakaway runner.* The concept for the secondary is always to rotate into pursuit; that is, they first back up and then circle towards the other side of the field. (See Figure 38.)

They must make aggressive tackles but always be under control. They are often the last defender and so a missed tackle will cost the team a high price. They generally want to edge to the outside of the runner, if possible, and force him inside, where there may be some more defensive help.

In a passing situation, the deep backs *always* look to intercept. They must expect to intercept, anticipate it, and try to catch the ball. The second biggest mistake they can make, however, is to *let a receiver get behind them.* They never want to let the receiver get too close to them, so that they will always have some room to react to a change of speed or direction.

4.

WHAT IS FOOTBALL ALL ABOUT?

Football is an intensely physical game in which two teams try to forcibly advance a ball against each other. It is played on a field that is 100 yards long and about 53 yards (160 feet) wide. The field is marked off in increments of 10 yards from the goal (or zero) yard line on one end, up to the 50 yard line across the center of the field, and down again to a goal line at the other end. There is a 10-yard end zone at each end of the field. (See Figure 39.)

The main idea is for one team, called the offense, to carry the ball into the other team's end zone, scoring a touchdown worth six points. The other team, called the defense, tries to stop them by tackling the ball-carrier and bringing him to the ground.

THE CONCEPT OF DOWNS

One of the toughest things for a parent or for people in general to understand about football is the concept of downs. Once a team gets possession of the ball, they must advance it at least 10 yards in four attempts. If they succeed, then they get four more attempts to go another 10 yards from the point of the last tackle.

Each attempt, or play, is called a *down*. Therefore, *first down and ten* means that the next play is the first of the four attempts and all 10 yards need to be made. Similarly, *third down and two* means that the next play is the third attempt in the series of four

Figure 39
DIMENSIONS OF A FOOTBALL FIELD
(Courtesy of NFSHSA.)

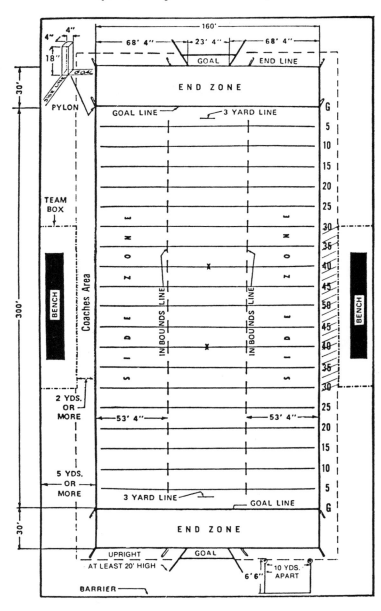

downs and 2 yards are still needed to make the 10 yards. If the offense gains 5 yards on the next play, then the team has succeeded and will maintain possession. They are awarded another first down. They therefore get four more attempts to advance another 10 yards, and so the next play is called first and ten again.

Stay with me! This is difficult for the beginner. Let's try once more! Suppose my son's team receives possession on a kickoff and they begin on their 20 yard line. They need to go 80 yards for a touchdown. However, the rules of football require only that the team worry about 10 yards at a time. His team has four chances to get the ball to the 30 yard line, so it's now first down and ten. If they advance to the 30 yard line in four plays they keep possession of the ball and get four more chances to go another 10 yards.

Okay, let's take it step by step back at the 20 yard line. Let's say our fullback carries the ball forward for 3 yards. Then the next play is referred to as *second down and seven* because it is the second try and they still need 7 yards to get to the 30 yard line. Then let us say that a pass play gains 5 more yards. So, now it's *third down and two* since the ball is on the 28 yard line after two attempts. Then my son catches a 9 yard pass. (Why not? It's my book!) Now the ball is on the 37 yard line. Since we passed the 30 yard line as originally required, we now have another *first down and 10* yards to go. The ball is on the 37 yard line and we have four tries to get it to the 47 yard line. However, suppose my son had dropped the ball. Then, it would be *fourth down and two* back on the 28 yard line. We have one more chance, and if we fail the other team gets the ball right there. Usually, since we are so near to our own goal line, we decide to punt (kick) the ball to the other team so that they will have farther to go for a score. That is why most teams punt on fourth down. Note that a team does not need to use all four plays to advance 10 yards. For instance, if it's first down and we pass for 20 yards, then it's first down again at the new spot.

MOVING THE BALL

Each team has eleven players on the field. The team with possession of the ball is called the offense and must have at least seven players spread along the line of scrimmage where the ball is. The line of scrimmage is an imaginary line that runs from the ball to each sideline. This leaves the quarterback and three other players who are running backs or wide receivers. The player in the center of the line hikes the ball back to the quarterback. (See Figure 40.) The ball may then be advanced by running it forward or by passing it to a player. A play is over when a ball-carrier's knee touches the ground (in youth ball), when a pass is not caught, or when the ball is run out of bounds.

A touchdown, worth six points, occurs when the team carries the ball across the goal line of the opposing team or catches a pass within the end zone. Scoring a touchdown also allows the team to attempt a point after touchdown—either kicking the ball through the uprights of the goalpost, worth one point, or carrying the ball across the goal line from a certain distance, worth two points. The latter is not allowed in the pro's; only a kick can be attempted. In youth ball, this scoring is reversed. Since kicked points are more difficult, two points are awarded, and running the ball across the goal line is worth one point.

Another way to score besides crossing the goal line is to place-kick the ball from the ground through the uprights of the goal post. This is called a field goal and scores three points. It usually occurs when the team with the ball faces a fourth down and the ball is within 30 yards of the end zone. If the coach feels that the odds are against getting another first down, he may try for a field goal. It rarely happens in pre-high school level of play.

That's Football!

Each team tries to score, and after a total of forty minutes of play (forty-eight in high school and sixty in the pro's), the team with the most points wins.

As a basic proposition the ball is hiked to the quarterback who then hands it off to a running back whose job is to advance the ball forward on the ground toward the goal line. The quarterback instead could pass it to a receiver who catches it and then tries to advance it farther. The quarterback may pass forward or sideways but he must be behind the scrimmage line when passing forward. The blockers try to interfere with the tacklers. They may push with the hands but cannot grab or hold the defense.

The idea for the defense is to tackle the ball-carrier or to prevent a pass by batting the ball away. The defense is free to move as they please just prior to the hike and may play quite fiercely. They may shift around to confuse the blockers. They may freely shove or throw blockers to one side with the hands. The use of the hands by

Figure 40
FOOTBALL, THE PLAY!

The center hikes the ball back to the quarterback. The seven linemen on the left block the defense on the right.

Figure 41
OFFSIDE

Note the ball still on the ground and two players have crossed the neutral zone. The defensive player could get back, but the end is offside.

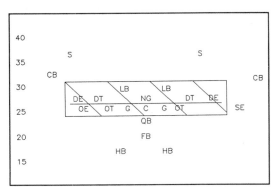

Figure 42
FREE BLOCKING ZONE

The free blocking zone is an area 8 yards wide by 6 yards deep, centered on the ball.

the defense against a blocker is virtually unlimited.

As a general rule, however, actions that are intended to hurt or maim, such as spearing with the helmet, punching in the head with a fist or forearm, grabbing a face mask, kicking or tripping, or jumping onto a pile of players, are considered to be serious infractions. These actions generally can lead to 15 yard unsportsmanlike conduct penalties or even an ejection from the game.

Now, there are many more rules. I will review the main ones. But, once you understand the concept of *downs*, then you know the essence of the game. The rest is detail. If you want all of the details then you should obtain a copy of the rules. Write to the National Federation of State High School Associations, 11724 Plaza Circle, P.O. Box 20626, Kansas City, MO 64195. For college rules write to the N.C.A.A. at P.O. Box 1906, Shawnee Mission, KS 66222.

My attempt here is to discuss the major rules so that they make sense to you. In doing so, I may omit certain nuances in an effort to promote your general understanding. In this regard, my review may be technically insufficient from time to time. Forgive me. Get a copy of the actual rules for technical precision; I'm just going to try and promote your general understanding here. The actual rules are worded quite technically, as they have to be to cover all sorts of situations. Here are some more of the major rules.

MAJOR RULES

1) **Offside** is an often called penalty covering several violations associated with players' actions at the moment of the hike. One example is called a *false start*. The basic idea is that offensive personnel must be in a ready or set position (e.g., hands on or near the ground) before the snap of the ball for a full second, and once in the set position the interior linemen may not move the hand or make any other sudden movement. The purpose for this rule is to protect the defense from being "pulled" across the line of scrimmage by the movement of a lineman, which would ordinarily signal that the play has begun. If an offensive lineman jerks, a defender will charge forward. Defenders are taught to move as soon as a lineman moves. So the offensive lineman cannot move until the ball is snapped. Another purpose of this rule is to make sure that the offensive player does not get any more of an edge than he already

Figure 43
POP WARNER AGE/WEIGHT SCHEMATIC

1988–89–90 POP WARNER TACKLE FOOTBALL AGE/WEIGHT SCHEMATIC

Division Name	Basic Ages	Additional Ages	Allowed When	Certification Weight Range	End of Season Maximum
		Player Born On Or After August 1st Current Year	Older/Lighter Player		
MITEY-MITE	7– 8– 9	10		40– 75 lbs.	81 lbs.**
(older/lighter)			10*	40– 55 lbs.	61 lbs.**
JUNIOR PEEWEE	8– 9–10	11		50– 85 lbs.	91 lbs.**
(older/lighter)			11*	50– 65 lbs.	71 lbs.**
PEEWEE	9–10–11	12		65–100 lbs.	106 lbs.**
(older/lighter)			12*	65– 80 lbs.	86 lbs.**
JUNIOR MIDGET	10–11–12	13		80–115 lbs.	121 lbs.**
(older/lighter)			13*	80– 95 lbs.	101 lbs.**
MIDGET	11–12–13	14		90–135 lbs.	141 lbs.**
(older/lighter)			14*	90–115 lbs.	121 lbs.**
SENIOR MIDGET	12–13–14	15		95–135 lbs.	141 lbs.**
(older/lighter)			15*	95–115 lbs.	121 lbs.**
JUNIOR BANTAM	12–13–14	15		110–150 lbs.	156 lbs.**
(older/lighter)			15*	110–130 lbs.	136 lbs.**
BANTAM	13–14–15	16		125–165 lbs.	171 lbs.**
(older/lighter)			16*	125–145 lbs.	151 lbs.**

*The asterisked (*) provisions in each division allow the so-called "overage, but underweight" player to also qualify, if born on or after August 1st of the prior year and not later than July 31st of the current year, thereby allowing the League Age to encompass four (4) years. However, the fourth year of eligibility (older/lighter player) falls under more stringent weight restrictions, per above.

**For all games played after Thanksgiving weekend, either Method A or Method B (see pages 23–24, Article 15, "In-Season Weight Increase") may be utilized, up to a maximum of seven (7) pounds.

has since he knows when the ball will be hiked. He cannot cross the line until the ball is hiked. Usually what happens is that a kid forgets the cadence number for the hike and leaves on "1", when the ball is not hiked until "2". (See Figure 42.)

The center, or snapper, may move the ball to get a grip on it, but may not pick it up, stand it up, or jerk his head or shoulder. The running backs must also be set for a full second before the ball is snapped, although one of them may be in motion sideways or backwards as the ball is snapped. An offensive player who is not set for the full second before the snap is said to be in *illegal motion*.

2) **Encroachment** is another form of *offside* and is generally the defensive version of it. However, it pertains to all players. Picture an imaginary line the length of the football between the two teams. It is called the neutral zone. No player except the center can have any part of his body in, on, or over this neutral zone when the ball is snapped. If a defender crosses this zone and gets back on his side without body contact before the ball is snapped, he is okay.

Remember, only the offensive interior linemen (the center, guard, and tackle) are frozen before the snap. The defense can be moving as much as they want, so long as they are not encroaching when the ball is snapped. As noted, the center—the snapper—may have his head or hand in the neutral zone, but not beyond it. Again, the basic idea here is to have everyone separated by at least the length of the ball before each play. Encroachment is a 5 yard penalty.

3) **Holding** is another penalty that is often called during a game. It is called against any player, but most often against an offensive lineman who uses his hands or arms to hook, lock, clamp, grasp, encircle, or hold in an effort to restrain an opponent (other than the runner). It is a 10 yard penalty and has taken the momentum out of many an offensive drive.

4) **Illegal blocking** is another major rule. You cannot block an opponent below the waist or clip him *except* in what is called a free blocking zone (4 yards laterally and 3 yards deep from the ball). (See Figure 42.)

5) **Legal blocking** occurs when clenched hands are in advance of the elbows but not extended more than 45 degrees from the body. If extended, the hands must be open and in front of the blocker's and opponent's frames. If the blocker makes initial legal contact above the waist and in front of the opponent, and then either slides down to below the waist or the opponent turns and continuous contact is made with his back, the block is legal.

6) **Pop Warner football.** Chances are your son will play Pop Warner football although there are other organizations as well. These rules sort out kids nicely according to weight and age groups with an eye towards insuring equality. It works well! Figure 43 is a schematic that sets forth the various groupings. Most leagues play the Pee Wee, Junior Midget, and Midget Groupings. (I wish they would change the names!) Older lighter means, for example, that a fourteen year old can play Midget Level ball, even though this is usually for eleven to thirteen year olds, if he weighs under 115 pounds. Every player must play at least four scrimmage plays per game. A kicked point after touchdown is worth two points while a pass or run into the endzone after a touchdown is only worth one point. Games are played for four ten-minute periods. The rules are strongly formulated to avoid running up big score differentials between the teams. Otherwise, the game is similar to the high school rules.

JARGON—TALKING FOOTBALL

Once you understand the concept of downs and some of the major rules, you know enough to be both an informed fan and a helpful parent. However, there is much more. I am not going to get down to all of the fine details, but there are a number of other things you should know. Take the time to read the following glossary. It will contain much in the way of rules, terms, and football jargon and will provide much insight into this all-American game.

ADORNMENTS — Uniform adornments that serve no purpose or are distracting are illegal. We see these from time to time in the pro's but not often at the youth level.

BACKFIELD—The quarterback and running backs constitute the offensive backfield. We have tailbacks (deep in the backfield), flanker backs (spread outside of the end), wingbacks (spread out behind the end), single or lone backs (when there is only one running back behind the quarterback), and others based on regional terminology. The defensive backfield is called the *secondary*.

BALL—The rules require a high school football to be a four paneled, pebbled-grain, tan cowhide with eight or twelve evenly spaced laces. It should be $10 \, 7/8$ to $11 \, 7/16$ inches long, with a $20 \, 3/4$ to $21 \, 1/4$ inch middle circumference and a $27 \, 3/4$ to $28 \, 1/2$ inch long circumference. It should weigh 14 to 15 ounces and is inflated to $12 \, 1/2$ to $13 \, 1/2$ pounds. At youth levels it can be a bit smaller in most dimensions. Thus the length can be 10 to 11 inches; mid-circumference can be 19 to 20 inches; the long circumference can be 26 to 27 inches; the weight can be 12 to 14 ounces; and inflation can be $12 \, 1/2$ to $13 \, 1/2$ pounds.

BAT—There are a few occasions when batting a ball by hand is legal. One can bat a pass, kick, or fumble in flight if he is attempting to block. He can also bat a kicked ball forward before it or he himself goes into the opponent's end zone to avoid a touchback.

BELLY—A deception move in which the quarterback holds the ball in the belly of a running back before withdrawing or releasing it. Thus the quarterback momentarily "rides the belly," and decides what to do based on what the defense does.

BLITZ—A defensive move by a member of the secondary (linebacker, cornerback, or safety) whereby he leaves his zone and rushes through a gap in the line to the quarterback, hoping to tackle him or the ball-carrier before they can adjust so that there is a loss of yardage. The move has some danger in that the blitzer's defensive zone is left exposed.

BLOCKING—The act of impeding a defensive player, moving him from the path of the ball-carrier or interfering with his ability to make a tackle. Types of blocks include: *cross blocks*, when two offensive linemen cross in front of each other and block each other's man; *cross body blocks*, in which a blocker hurls his body horizontally across the chest of a defender; *shoulder blocks*, or jolts; *open field blocks*, in which one blocks a defender downfield; and *screens*, in which one simply gets between a defender and the ball-carrier. A running back who blocks well is often called a blocking back. One also endeavors to *block* or bat punts and place-kicks.

BOOTLEG — A deception move whereby the quarterback fakes a hand-off to a running back and then, hiding the ball by his hip, runs wide around the end to gain yardage. Often the run will initially be a casual one in which the quarterback pretends he doesn't have the ball to perpetuate the fake, and then he suddenly speeds up.

BUCK—Running hard into the middle of the line, often on a short yardage situation.

BUTTONHOOK—The receiver runs straight ahead for 5-7 yards, then wheels and turns to face the quarterback for a pass. It is often a timing pass and the ball meets him as soon as he stops and turns. A great fake move here if the quarterback has time is for the receiver to break downfield just after the defender approaches. It's

Figure 44
BUTTONHOOK

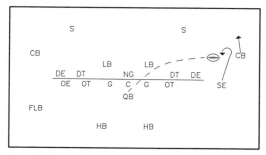

An all-time favorite, the receiver runs about 5 yards at top speed to get the defender moving backward and then suddenly stops and turns toward the passer for the pass.

a bread and butter touchdown play, if the quarterback has time to let the fake occur. (See Figure 44.)

CENTER—The offensive lineman who snaps (or centers) the ball to the quarterback. He is usually found in the center of the offensive line. The center generally has a number in the 50's.

CHAIN GANG—No, they are not criminals. At youth levels they are parents who are pressed into service along the sideline. One is responsible for holding the down marker, a tall pole with cards displayed on the top to signify which down it is. This person places the pole on the new line of scrimmage on each play. Two more parents man the chains, which are two tall poles separated by a 10-foot chain. The distance between these poles is the distance that must be covered to get a first down.

CHEERLEADERS—These young girls work every bit as hard as the players, during practices and games. They add much to the spirit of competition and to what football is all about.

CLIPPING—A serious penalty in which a player blocks an opponent from behind and below the waist outside of a free blocking zone (see below). It is a 15 yard penalty. If the block is above the waist it's only 5 yards and is called *illegal use of the hands*.

COUNTER—A play design whereby the offensive backs flow in one direction, then one cuts back to run the ball in the other direction.

CUTBACK—A runner's move when he crosses the line of scrimmage in a certain direction and then cuts back in the other direction as he penetrates the defense. It's like a counter except that it occurs spontaneously and after he crosses the line of scrimmage.

DEAD BALL SPOT—The dead ball spot is the spot under the foremost point of the ball when it becomes dead by rule; that is, when the runner steps on or over the sideline or when his knee touches the ground. In the pro's, it is when his knee touches the ground as a result of contact with an opponent. If they slip in the pro's, they can get up again and run if they were not touched. The place where the official spots the ball is often a source of sideline grumbling, since it can often decide whether a team will keep the ball or lose possession.

DEFENSE—The attempt to stop the other team from scoring or advancing the ball.

DIVE—A running play up the middle in the gap between the center and the guard. It is a quickly moving play that is usually run by a strong back, the fullback.

DOUBLE-TEAM—When a defender is very strong and is giving the offense too much trouble, two blockers will be assigned to double-team him in a coordinated block.

DOWN—A down is a play. A team gets four of these to move the ball 10 yards. If they succeed, they get four more plays. If they fail, the other team gets the ball. On fourth down, a team will usually punt (kick) the ball to the other team so that they will have farther to go for the score. However, when the offense is near the goal line, they usually either run a play to get a first down or kick a field goal.

DRAW—This is a play that tries to draw the defense into the backfield. It is done by delaying the hand-off to the running back. Then, as a defender charges, he is hit in the side by a pre-designed trap block and the runner is then free to advance. The delay is needed to give the blocker time to pull and get to the defender.

DROP KICK—This is not used much anymore since place-kicks are now universally considered to be the best way to kick field goals and points-after-touchdown. In the olden days, on a drop kick the kicker would drop the ball on its tip point and kick it immediately as it began to bounce up. It is tricky to do, and so most teams sacrifice a potential blocker to hold the ball.

DUMMY—These are players who hold dummy or blocking pads in practice to allow blockers to run through their plays and work on blocking form.

ENCROACHMENT — Having any part of the body inside the neutral zone at the snap of the ball.

END—The offensive or defensive player who positions himself at either end of the front line. On offense, if in close to the rest of the line, it's a tight end; otherwise it's a split end. They usually have a number in the 80's.

END ZONE—The area covering 10 yards past the goal line. If a pass is caught in the end zone it is a touchdown. The goal posts are located at the back of the end zone.

EQUIPMENT—Pop Warner and National Federation rules require a N.O.C.S.A.E. certified helmet with a visible warning label, a properly fastened chin strap, a multiple bar face protector of non-breakable material, shoulder pads, hip pads with tailbone protector, thigh guards, kneepads, mouth guard with a keeper strap, and an athletic supporter. I think that the boys should also wear a cup, sanctioned forearm pads and shin guards, and neck braces, but they are not required as of now. Kids may not wear any hard substance such as casts or knee braces unless all of the hard surface is covered by 1/2-inch thick, closed cell, slow recovery rubber.

EXTRA POINT—At youth levels, the point after touchdown may be attempted from the 3 yard line. If the ball is place-kicked through the goal post upright, two points are scored in Pop Warner play.

FAIR CATCH—By raising his hand above his head quickly and clearly, a player may receive a punt or place-kick without being tackled. He may not, however, advance the ball and a muffed catch results in a live ball.

FIELD GOAL—When a team has a fourth down and is close to the goal line, they can opt to place-kick the ball through the uprights for three points. It doesn't happen often at the youth level because the kids don't place-kick with accuracy yet.

FIRST DOWN—The first in each series of four downs to move the ball 10 yards.

FLAG—The yellow penalty cloth that officials keep in their back pocket and throw in the air designating a rule violation. It is the bane of coaches and fans, after a 50-yard touchdown run, to look upfield and see that yellow flag on the field near the line of scrimmage, usually signifying a holding penalty and an erasure of the score.

FLEA FLICKER—The quarterback hands off to a running back who then flicks the ball *back* to the quarterback for a pass play. It fools the defense, which thinks that it is a running play and thus they leave pass receivers unguarded.

FORWARD PASS—A ball may be thrown forward from behind the line of scrimmage to an eligible receiver (an end or a back). Once past the line of scrimmage, a ball may only be thrown laterally or backwards.

FORWARD PROGRESS — This represents the point at which the ball will be placed after a play, marking the forward-most point of a runner's progress before he was involuntarily knocked backward. If a receiver backs up voluntarily he loses any forward progress that he had gained beyond the point of the tackle.

FREE BLOCKING ZONE—A rectangular area extending 4 yards laterally and 3 yards forward and behind each scrimmage line from the point of the ball. In this zone an offensive player who was stationary at the snap and any defensive player may contact an opponent below the waist or from the rear.

FULLBACK—A running back. Usually he is the strongest running back, used for short yardage dives up the middle. Fullbacks usually have numbers in the 30's.

FUMBLE—Dropping the football before the play ends. It usually occurs upon a hard tackle. A fumble cannot be caused by contact with the ground. A fumble is a live ball and whoever recovers it gains possession.

GAPS—The spaces between offensive linemen through which the ball is carried. Defensemen must think of filling the gaps.

GOAL LINE—The thick white lines marking the ends of the 100-yard playing surface. If any point of the ball breaks the plane of this line, it is a touchdown.

GOAL POSTS—The goal is the vertical plane that extends above the crossbar and between the uprights of the goal posts, situated in the center of the end line, at each end of the field. The crossbar is 10 feet above the ground and is 23 feet, 4 inches long. The upright may be 4 inches thick and extend no less than 10 feet above the crossbar. The lower goal post or posts shall be padded. A wind directional streamer may be atop one of the uprights.

GUARD—An interior lineman on offense who lines up next to the center. The middle person on the defensive line is called a nose guard. They usually wear numbers in the 60's.

HALFBACKS—The faster running backs. Usually lined up behind and to one side of the quarterback for wide running plays. They usually wear numbers in the 40's.

HALFTIME — After two ten-minute quarters (at the Pop Warner level) there is a fifteen-minute halftime break. The pro's recently reduced this break to twelve minutes to speed up the game.

HASH MARKS—Also called the inbound line, these markings are 24 inches in length and form two broken lines down the field, 53 feet, 4 inches from each sideline, and divide the field longitudinally into thirds. When a ball goes out of bounds or is downed near a sideline, it is centered on the nearest hash mark. This gives the team some running room to each side on every play.

HUDDLE—The players gather before each play in a circle or other regular formation to receive the play instructions from the quarterback.

Figure 45
KICKOFF

The game begins with one team—here the team on the right—kicking off to the other team. Kickoffs also occur after touchdowns and field goals.

INCOMPLETION—A forward pass that is not caught or not possessed by the receiver for a full step.

INELIGIBLE RECEIVER—Only the ends or backs may be downfield to receive a pass. This penalty often occurs on punts when an interior lineman breaks downfield before the ball is punted.

INTERCEPTION—A pass reception by the defense. It's the dream and the glory of the defensive back.

INTERFERENCE—It can be called against the offense or defense for interfering with a player who is trying to receive a pass, usually by bumping or grabbing his hands before the ball gets to him. Incidental contact between two players who are both looking at and trying to catch a pass is not interference. The judgment is always whether the player was playing the receiver or the ball.

KICKOFF—This is the free kick that starts the game and the second half. It also occurs after each touchdown or successful field goal and is kicked from the kicking team's 40 yard line. A kickoff return is the formation used by the receiving team to return the ball. (See Figure 45.)

LATERAL—A sideways or backwards pass. It can be thrown at any time from any place on the field and usually is used to avoid a tackle.

LINEBACKERS — The defensive personnel immediately behind defensive linemen. They are usually both agile and strong, and they are great tacklers. They often wear numbers in the 50's or 90's.

MAN-TO-MAN—A pass defense term that designates individual coverage. Each defensive back is assigned to stay with a specific offensive receiver on a pass play.

MIDFIELD—The 50 yard line, marked by a stripe across the center of the field. The seats on the 50 yard line are considered to be the best in the house.

MUFF—An unsuccessful attempt to recover a fumble.

NEUTRAL ZONE—An imaginary belt across the field formed by the nose tip and back point of the football as it rests with its foremost tip on the line of scrimmage.

OFFENSE — The team with possession of the ball; they attempt to advance the ball and score.

OFFICIALS — There are usually four men in a high school crew. I've seen Pop Warner games with only two or three. The *referee* is in charge—he keeps score and generally supervises the conduct of the game and keeps the game clock. He decides differences of opinion. He usually lines up on the offensive side of scrimmage and primarily decides forward progress of the ball. The *umpire* is responsible for penalty administration and lines up on the defensive side of scrimmage. The *linesman* covers action in the neutral zone and stands on the line of scrimmage. He also looks for pass interference in his side of the field. The *line judge* is on the opposite side of the field from the linesman. The official signals are found in Figure 46.

OFFSIDE—A penalty received for crossing the line of scrimmage before the ball is snapped.

OFF-TACKLE—The gap between the tackle and the end and a popular place for running plays.

OPTION — A popular play at youth and high school levels, even in some colleges. A quarterback sweeps around an end with another running back just off his outside shoulder. He can keep the ball or lateral it to the other back depending on how the defense reacts. An option pass play is a sweep by a halfback who has the option of passing the ball or continuing the run, again depending on how the defense reacts. We now see *triple option* plays that include an optional belly dive before the option sweep.

Figure 46
OFFICIAL SIGNALS

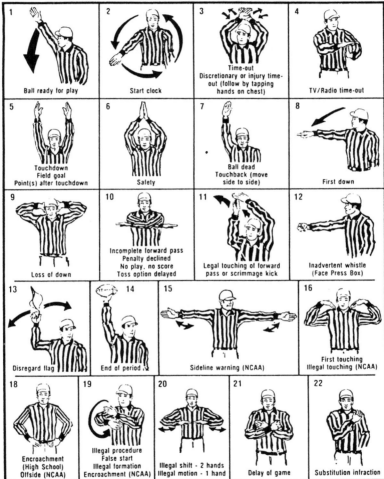

Figure 46 cont'd
OFFICIAL SIGNALS

OFFICIAL FOOTBALL SIGNALS
HIGH SCHOOL AND COLLEGE

23 Failure to wear required equipment	**24** Illegal helmet contact	**27** Unsportsmanlike conduct Noncontact foul	**28** Illegal participation
29 Sideline interference (NCAA)	**30** Running into (NCAA) or Roughing Kicker or Holder	**31** Illegal batting Illegal kicking (Followed by pointing toward toe for kicking)	**32** Invalid fair catch signal (High School) Illegal fair catch signal	**33** Forward pass interference Kick catching interference
34 Roughing passer	**35** Illegal pass Illegal forward handing	**36** Intentional grounding	**37** Ineligible downfield on pass	**38** Personal foul
39 Clipping	**40** Blocking below waist Illegal block	**41** Chop block	**42** Holding or obstructing	**43** Illegal use of hands or arms
44 Helping runner Interlocked blocking	**45** Grasping face mask or helmet opening	**46** Tripping	**47** Player disqualification

PENALTIES—According to the National Federation of State High Schools Association rules, the following penalties call for a loss of yards.

Summary of Penalties

A) Loss of 5 Yards.
1. Failure to properly wear required equipment during a down.
2. Delay of game.
3. Failure to properly wear required equipment just before the snap.
4. Illegal substitution.
5. Encroachment.
6. Free kick infraction.
7. Invalid or illegal fair catch signal.
8. False start or any illegal act by snapper.
9. Fewer than seven players on the offensive line or a numbering violation.
10. Illegal formation or procedure at snap.
11. Illegal motion or shift.
12. Illegal handling ball forward (also loss of down).
13. Illegal forward pass (if by offense, loss of down also).
14. Intentional grounding (also loss of down).
15. Ineligible receiver downfield.
16. Helping runner.
17. Attendant illegally on field.
18. Non-player outside of the team box but not on field.

B) Loss of 10 yards.
1. Illegal blocking technique.
2. Illegal use of hands.
3. Interlocked blocking.
4. Holding.
5. Runner grasping a teammate.
6. Striking blocker's head with hand(s).

C) Loss of 15 yards.
1. Fair catch interference.
2. Illegal block after valid or invalid fair catch signal.
3. Forward pass interference (also loss of down if by offense; a first down if by defense). If intentional or unsportsmanlike, an additional 15 yards.
4. Illegal block below the waist or on free kicker or holder.

5. Clipping.
6. Chop block.
7. Tripping.
8. Charging into an opponent obviously out of the play.
9. Piling, hurdling, unnecessary roughness, and other personal fouls.
10. Grasping an opponent's face protector (or any helmet opening).
11. Butt block, face tackle, or spear.
12. Roughing the passer (also a first down).
13. Roughing the kicker or holder (also a first down).
14. Unsportsmanlike conduct by player or non-player.
15. Illegal participation.
16. Illegal kicking or batting the ball.
17. Non-player illegally on field.

D) Disqualification associated with certain 15 yard penalties.
1. Striking, kicking, kneeing.
2. Any act if unduly rough or flagrant.

PILE-UP—It is illegal to pile upon a tackled ballplayer. However, the forward momentum of tacklers often carries several to a pile-up. (See Figure 47.)

PITCHOUT—A play designed to get a halfback to the outside very quickly. On a sweep play the ball is pitched to him as he darts to the outside. (See Figure 48.)

PLACE-KICK—Kicking a ball in a kickoff, a field goal, or a point after touchdown when the ball is held in place for a teammate.

PLATOON—Having different players on the offensive team than those on the defense. At youth levels the best players will play both ways.

POCKET—An area formed by the offensive pass blockers in front and to the side of the quarterback in a pass play.

POINT AFTER TOUCHDOWN—A team may score one or two additional points after a touchdown. At youth levels two are scored on a place-kick between the uprights, and one is scored on a rush or pass into the end zone. The line of scrimmage for P.A.T. is the 3 yard line.

POST—The post pass is a deep one across the middle, toward the goal post. It's also called a Hail Mary or a bomb.

PUNT—A ball kicked to the opponent by dropping it onto

Figure 47
PILE-UP

Pile-ups are part of the romp and tumble of the game.

Figure 48
PITCHOUT

Here the quarterback pitched the ball in the nick of time.

Figure 49
SHOESTRING TACKLE

Many a touchdown has been saved by a diving tackle grabbing the runner at the shoestrings.

the foot. This usually is the method for exchanging possession on fourth down.

PURSUIT—The defensive act of pursuing the ball-carrier on an intercept angle, even if the play goes away from the defender.

QUARTER—The game is divided into four time periods called quarters, usually ten minutes each at pre-high school levels. There is a one- to two-minute period between quarters and a fifteen-minute halftime. High school games are for four twelve-minute quarters.

QUARTERBACK—The offensive captain and field general who calls the plays. He takes the snap and hands off the ball to a running back or he passes it. Usually he will wear a number between 1 and 19.

RAZZLE-DAZZLE—Intricate or funny play patterns such as end around, reverse, flea flicker, or option. They involve tricky hand-offs and often take a lot of precision, but can break for big plays.

REPLAY—Videocameras used only in the pro's to review an official's call. They are not used at any other level and are a matter of some controversy.

REVERSE—A razzle-dazzle play in which a running back runs to one side, pulling the defense with him and then hands off the ball to another player going the other way.

ROLL-OUT — Instead of staying in the pass protection "pocket," an agile quarterback can run off to one side to gain time for his receivers to get free for a pass. This is a *scramble* if not designed ahead of time.

SACK—Tackling a quarterback behind the line of scrimmage. This is the dream of every pass rusher.

SAFETY — The deepest defensive back. Also a tackle in a team's own end zone resulting in two points and a free kick to the opponent.

SCRAMBLE — When a quarterback's protection breaks down, he often has to scramble away from onrushing tacklers.

SCREEN PASS—A play that allows the defensive line to rush the quarterback freely, as a ploy. The quarterback then lofts a short pass over the charging defenders to a receiver who lines up just behind the waiting offensive linemen.

SCRIMMAGE—The imaginary line across the field that runs through the point of the front tip of the ball; also a practice foot ball game.

SECONDARY—The defensive backfield.

SHIFT—Offensive backs and defenders are allowed to shift position and change alignment, individually or as a unit, before the ball is snapped. Offensive players must be set for one second before the snap (one player may legally be in motion).

SHIVER—A useful defensive weapon, thrusting the hands forward, palms forward, into a blocker's shoulders to keep him at bay and thus not allowing him access to the defender's body.

SHOESTRING TACKLE—We like to tackle hard with the shoulder, but when the ball-carrier is breaking away we take what we can get. (See Figure 49.)

SHOTGUN—An offensive formation in which the quarterback lines up 4 to 5 yards behind the center to receive the snap. This is used on obvious passing situations and helps the quarterback gain a few seconds. Since he need not drop back, he can more readily focus on the secondary and the pass pattern.

SIDELINES—The white stripe lengthwise down the sides of the field. This line is out of bounds to any body part.

SIGNALS—The hiking cadence and instructions called by a quarterback at the line of scrimmage. A typical one is "Down—Green—242—Set—Hike 1—Hike 2—Hike 3." "Down" signifies that the team should get in the ready position. "Green" is a code that signals if the play will be changed and is followed by the new play. The "set" signal gets the linemen into set position. The ball is hiked on a number called in the huddle.

SLANT—A block to one side, or a running play off-tackle or off-guard.

SNAP—The backward hike of the ball from the center between his legs to the quarterback or other person (punter, place-kick holder).

SPIN—A nifty move by a running back as he is about to be tackled. A good spin often can break free from a mediocre tackle.

STANCE—The position of any player upon the snap of the ball. Stances are designed to ready a person for his particular job and vary according to that task.

STRAIGHT-ARM—A useful weapon for a running back is to stiff arm, palms outward, onto the shoulder of a would-be tackler. A "hop" upon contact can often launch a runner, using the tackler's momentum, for several feet.

STUNTS—Defensive moves to confuse blocking assignments by having linemen switch charging lanes upon the snap of the ball.

SUBMARINE—A low, diving, defensive line move to get under a block and into a gap. The player then pulls his legs up quickly to meet the ball-carrier.

SUBSTITUTION — The substitution rules are fairly unrestricted. Any number of players may enter or leave between downs. No more than eleven players may be on the field at one time, although less is not illegal. Eleven players are needed to start, but not finish, a game in high school.

SWEEP — A running play that heads wide laterally and endeavors to run around the defense.

TACKLE—A lineman on offense or defense who plays inside the end. They are usually the biggest players on the team and their numbers are in the 70's. This term also designates the art of bringing a ball-carrier to his knees.

TAILBACK—The deepest running back.

TIME OUT—Any side may stop the clock after any play three times per half. This is usually done by a team in possession of the ball to delay the half from ending so that they have a chance to score. It's also used to talk things over before an important play. In youth levels it's used a lot to stop the twenty-five second clock from expiring while waiting for a sleeping ten year old to get back onto the field.

TIMING PASS — A pre-arranged pass pattern in which the quarterback throws to an area before the receiver actually turns (or stops). It is usually too sophisticated for most youth teams.

TOUCHBACK — A punt or kickoff that goes into the end zone and is downed there by the team who will take possession. A touchback also occurs when a fumbled ball is recovered or a pass is intercepted in the offensive end zone by the defense and no attempt is made to run it out. They then get the ball on the 20 yard line.

TOUCHDOWN — Breaking the plane of the goal line with the ball. This can be achieved by running the ball over the goal line or catching a pass in the end zone. It is the primary objective of football and scores six points. (See Figure 50.)

TRAPPING—Blocking a player from the side after allowing him to advance beyond the line of scrimmage.

UNBALANCED LINE — An offensive line with more line

Figure 50
TOUCHDOWN

The name of the game!

Figure 51
WATERBOY

Usually a future ball-player or a watching parent.

men on one side of the center than on the other.

WATERBOY—There are a lot of sideline jobs and this is one of the most important to avoid dehydration on a hot day. (See igure 51.)

WINGBACK—A running back who lines up outside of the offensive end.

ZONE DEFENSE—When the pass defense protects a certain territory rather than defending man-to-man.

5.

CONCEPTS, FORMATIONS, PATTERNS

Here is where it starts to get complicated. We earlier discussed one difference between football and other sports in that it involves more desire than skill. (Please understand, I do not mean this disparagingly; desire is just of greater importance.) Another major difference is that the action on the field is much more controlled compared to other sports. Each offensive play is fully and precisely diagrammed and repeatedly practiced. Boys will line up on the practice field and run through play patterns endlessly. They will be expected to run plays smoothly. Blocking assignments are carefully planned out and passing routes are measured to the step.

Other sports have play patterns, but not as precisely worked out as in football. Basketball has specific offensive patterns, but there is much more flexibility. Soccer is at the other extreme and flows more according to general motion concepts. In football, play is largely pre-programmed, although players also need to be able to react to some extent to the situation at hand, as in all sports.

It is not the purpose of this book to get too deeply into the most complex aspects of the game. This chapter will discuss some general offensive and defensive *concepts*. It will also describe some specific formations and play patterns used in youth football so that you can gain a working sense of what's going on. It will be of great help to your child to discuss the *underlying concepts* of offensive and defensive play with you. It will help him to open and broaden his perception regarding what's going on around him. Once a player understands why things are done a certain way, he can perform more intelligently.

OFFENSIVE CONCEPTS

Control Possession of the Ball

The bread and butter play of basketball, as mentioned in my book *A Parent's Guide to Coaching Basketball*, is to feed the big man under the hoop for a power shot. If you can do this successfully and repeatedly, you will win. Well, the bread and butter play of football is the *power running play*—the dive up the middle or the slant off-tackle.

If a team can successfully and consistently run the ball and slowly chew up yardage, gaining 4 or 5 yards per play, then they will use up a lot of time. This means that the other team will have the ball themselves for less time. At youth levels, a good drive down the field, let's say 70 yards, will take about fifteen plays and can consume an entire quarter of play. *The other team can't score if they don't have the ball!* Luck is a large part of football, as in any sport, and teams often get lucky and break a big play 50 yards for a score. But if you reduce the amount of time that the other team possesses the ball, you will reduce the odds of their making such a play.

At the Pop Warner level, football is much more of a running game than it is later on. However, as mentioned earlier, the big running plays are often wide sweeps by a really fast kid who just outruns everyone and breaks away for a score. Yet, the more conservative run up the middle is the cornerstone of good offense.

On first down the idea is to run a slant between the tackle and the end and get 5 yards. Then we have two more shots at the next 5 yards. If your son's team can do this regularly, they will be quite successful.

Open a Hole; Penetrate the Defensive Line

Mother Nature has a rule: solid matter can't penetrate solid matter. If we want to advance the football, we need to open a hole in the defensive wall so the runner can get by. Therefore, the primary objective of every running play is to get the ball-carrier through the first line of defense. If we do that, we will make at

Figure 52
OPEN A HOLE

The offense has opened up a nice hole on the right side. Note the double-team slant block on #52.

least our 4 to 5 yards, and perhaps our runner will have time *to put a move* on the defensive secondary and get more yardage.

Sure, a really strong kid can block a defensive lineman who is ahead of him and just shove him out of the way, creating a hole. However, the kids are usually of similar strength, so we have to get smart. The key to opening a hole consistently is usually in *slant blocking.* (See Figure 52.)

If we can get our blockers into position where they are attacking their target defender from an angle, their job will be much easier. It's tough to block big, strong defensive tackles head on. They are usually the strongest players in the game. So, if we can approach them from the side, we will avoid their strength. Plays are usually designed to provide as much slant blocking as possible.

Lead the Play Through the Hole

Often we get a hole opened up on the line, but a linebacker or defensive secondary player eludes a blocker and heads to the hole. It is very tough to make that initial block on the linebacker, so they will often get to the hole when they see it forming. The offensive response is to have someone *lead the play through the hole.* We send a blocker into the hole ahead of the ball-carrier to block out the first defender who gets to the hole. We usually send a blocking back or pull a guard to do this job.

If all of these efforts fail and the hole is not opened, or perhaps it closes very quickly, then the runner is on his own. He can try to bull his way through for a yard or two, or change direction and try his luck elsewhere, just looking for daylight.

Run on Short Yardage; Throw on Long Yardage

If it is third down and 2 yards to go for a first down, the odds are that we can pick up the 2 yards with a power play diving up the middle with our strongest running back, usually the fullback. However, if it's third down and 9, or let's say we got a penalty and it's second down and 19, then we have a long way to go. Since running plays usually average only several yards each, the odds are better to throw the ball in long yardage situations. A pass play can get 10 to 15 yards—much more if the receiver can make a move and avoid the first tackler.

Screen or Draw a Rushing Defense

We noted earlier that a defender's primary job is usually to control his area. There is a passive aspect that just says, "Don't let anybody get by." However, sometimes a defense gets ahead of itself and finds that they can easily penetrate the offensive line to get into the offensive backfield. This is disaster for the offense. A good coach will spot this and use the defensive momentum to help his team, much like the concepts of the martial arts, which use an attacker's momentum to one's own advantage.

In such a circumstance, a screen play should be tried. The blockers give the rushing defenders a jolt just to slow them up and then let them go. The quarterback drops back and then lofts a soft, short pass over the onrushing defense to a receiver who now has the blockers in front of him.

Trap blocks are also useful against onrushing defenders in a *draw play*. Here, the running back hesitates a second to give a

Figure 53
TRAP BLOCK ON A DRAW PLAY

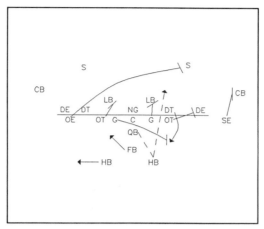

*The defensive tackle comes across
toward the right halfback and is
trapped by the left guard.*

Figure 54
SWEEP AROUND END

*A lot of touchdowns in youth football are scored by a
speedster outrunning everyone wide around the end.*

pulling lineman time to get to his blocker. Then the quarterback hands off the ball and, just as the tackler thinks he will make a big tackle in the backfield, he is creamed from the side and taken out of the play. (See Figure 53.)

Misdirection

Another useful play concept is to sweep the backs in one direction to get the defense moving that way, then hand off to one back who counters against the flow. The blockers then have it easier since the motion pulls the defense to lean away from the actual play. However, if the defense is keying on the linemen and not the backs, this will not work as well.

Sweep Your Speedster

A coach must go with the hand he is dealt. If he has a super-fast running back, then he will have the opportunity to run him wide around the whole pack. Again, the main idea is to get past the defensive line and get that all-so-valuable 4 to 5 yards per carry. So, one way to get past the line is simply to run around it. A pitchout is a play designed to do just that. The speedster lines up off-tackle and immediately darts outside upon the snap. The quarterback quickly laterals or pitches the ball underhand to the speedster, who then sprints to the sideline and tries to turn the corner and get some yardage. On such a play he is on his own. No blockers will get out fast enough to help much. It's just speed against speed. If a coach is blessed enough to have someone with such speed, the sweep play becomes a great tool. (See Figure 54.)

Spread Out the Defense

When a team runs up the middle a lot, the defense will tend to bunch up in the middle. Thus the coach will need to open them up a bit. Putting a few wide receivers split out along the line of scrimmage will help. Running a sweep or some pass plays will also spread out the linebackers and secondary.

Take It to the Airways

There are few passes thrown at the youth level. The kids don't catch as well, the passes are not accurate, and pass blocking is usually poor (for reasons I can't understand, since pass blocking is the easiest thing in football). A passing game is usually dangerous and there is a high potential for interceptions. The toughest part about youth passing seems to be the timing. Quarterbacks tend to hold the ball too long. *They don't hit the receiver when he is in the seam,* that is, in an open area between defenders. How often I have seen a kid wide open across the middle, but the quarterback doesn't pass the ball until the receiver reaches the deep coverage and is thus no longer free.

In any event, if a team is up against a tough defense and cannot run the ball, they have to go to the air and hope to get lucky. It can happen.

I believe the most effective passes at the youth level are passes to the tight end in the flat, crossing behind a wide receiver who slants in. (See Figure 55.) For some reason this area is often open. The deep bomb is a dangerous play, and passes across the middle usually find a lot of congestion. But a screen—a short pass to the flat—is a good tool, particularly if the quarterback has speed and can roll out. If the pass is across the middle, I recommend very quick, short passes. The quarterback doesn't even drop back but tosses it over the middle to a big tight end who finds some open space. It must be very quick. The backs both head to each side of the center to stop a blitz and/or freeze the linebacker. (See Figure 56.)

Razzle-Dazzle

It's a fancy term—an over-glorified term that usually means a team can't overpower the defense and has to resort to complicated plays like reverses or flea flickers. A reverse is a play in which the quarterback hands off to one running back going wide, and he in turn hands off to another player going the opposite way. The idea is to get the defense going one way and then to have a speedster suddenly switch the other way around the whole pack. A flea flicker is a play in which the quarterback hands off to a running back who takes a few steps forward and then turns and flicks the ball back to the quarterback, who then throws a long pass. The idea is to get the defensive backs to think it's a running play and thus come forward, while a receiver scampers past them for the long pass. There are also option plays. Razzle-dazzle can break open a big play, but it can also lead to a big loss when the defense is not outsmarted. The plays take a long time to execute, and a lot can go wrong. We don't see too much of this action in youth football.

DEFENSIVE CONCEPTS

There is a special feeling, a strong pride, that comes from being a defensive ballplayer. Sure, the offensive backs get more glory, but even that is changing a bit as the great linebackers like Lawrence Taylor and Bruce Smith achieve recognition. Most athletes who have played the game have their fondest memories of the defensive play. We have pointed out repeatedly in this book that the essence of football is the desire to overcome an opponent. Defense is made for this! It is more free since one may have fuller, nearly unlimited, use of the hands, whereas offensive players are significantly more constrained. Defense is mainly blood and guts, let me at 'em, clawing, scraping, head knocking, gritty, thumping football! However, there are some general concepts that find their way through all the sound and fury, and they are most helpful to understand. Talk them over with your son.

Look for the Keys

Defenders are always sensitive to tips or hints on where the play will go, as we discussed earlier. However, the best defensive tool, particularly at the youth level where things are less complicated, is to play the motion or flow of the offense, focusing particularly on certain players such as the offensive guard. There are a few very specific keys to look for:

A) If the guard does not charge forward but steps back a bit in a stationary position, he is pass-blocking, and it's a pass play.

B) If he crosses the line of scrimmage, it's a running play, probably up the middle.

C) If he pulls in either direction, it's a running play in that direction.

The defensive backs can generally rely upon these keys to help them quickly react and know what type of play is occurring.

Go with the Flow

The flow of a play shows itself instantly. The whole team suddenly shifts one way or the other, and the defense must respond

Figure 55
PASS TO THE FLAT

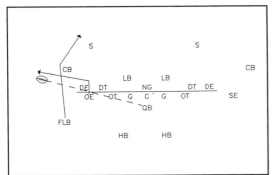

The wide receiver, here a flanker back, takes the cornerback deep, and so the tight end should be free in the flat.

Figure 56
QUICK SLANT PASS

The tight end slants directly across the middle with a very quick dash and grabs a pass. The quarterback doesn't even drop back, but just throws quickly.

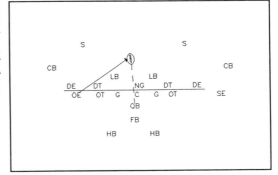

Figure 57
PURSUIT

The three defensive backs are engaging in a nice pursuit angle, with the last man #34 taking the deepest angle.

immediately. The first two steps are the most critical to react to and get out in front of the flow, thus reducing the advantage of surprise the offense has with their knowledge of the timing of the snap.

Pressure the Middle

The offensive team that can drive up the middle for 4 or 5 yards a play will dominate the game and will keep the other team's offense off the field. It follows then that the primary job of the defense is to shut down the power running game. Youth teams will put their strongest players up the middle on defense. Once you bang back a few dive plays, the offense will have to go to lower percentage plays like sweeps or passes. It's much easier to stop a sweep or pass since they are more complicated to execute, and so the defense has time to get more people on the job. The offense has to rely much more on execution to pull wide plays off. However, up the middle is power territory. *The team that controls the middle of the line has a decided advantage.*

Contain and Force the Play Inside

In soccer, we force the ball outside, wide away from the goal. In football, however, we want to deny daylight to the runner. The idea is to keep the runner inside where there is always more defensive help. The primary job of the defensive end—or outside linebacker, depending on the formation — is *to turn the wide running play inside*. Cornerbacks likewise are told to approach the man from the outside and turn him in where teammates are hopefully in pursuit. Most of the big gains on running plays come when a back can somehow get by the outside man and then sprint down the sideline.

Pursuit

How often during a youth game do you see defensive personnel standing and watching a play that goes to the opposite side? It causes me to wonder whether coaches at youth levels teach this concept enough. I know when I played that the instinct to take a little rest when the action went the other way was quite strong. However, a significant number of times the action turns back, and so *pursuing can lead to a big tackle and save a touchdown.* Furthermore, the play could turn the far corner, and often the pursuing defender can take an angle that meets the runner downfield. (See

Figure 58
STUNTS

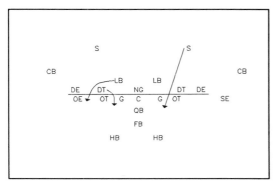

Two stunts are performed here. On the left a tackle and linebacker exchange positions, the tackle slanting in and the linebacker looping around. On the right a safety blitz occurs through the inside tackle hole.

Figure 57.) Of course a defender cannot get into pursuit if he is entangled with his blocker. This is why it is so important to keep the blocker away from the body, using the hands to push or shiver him away, shed him, and then engage in pursuit of the ball-carrier. Kids must be told to keep moving until the whistle blows. If the play goes the other way they must chase it, laterally at first to ensure against a reverse. Then they must head downfield at an angle that seems reasonable and run until they hear a whistle. Good pursuit wins close games.

Stunts

Defensive linemen and linebackers have a certain zone to defend. However, sometimes their primary positions are changed to confuse offensive blocking assignments. A stunt is a defensive play in which responsibilities are swapped. A defensive tackle, usually responsible for the outside shoulder area of his opponent, will slant diagonally inside while the inside linebacker loops around him to cover the off-tackle play. (See Figure 58.) Stunts can confuse offensive blockers and often result in easy tackles. However, a slip-up here can also play into the hands of the offense. That tackle could get blocked on a dive up the middle, and the linebacker will have taken himself out of the play.

Another stunt that is often very effective is the blitz. One or more of the defensive secondary leave their positions and crash forward into the line. Again, these plays are quite often successful

Figure 59
THE SACK

Nothing adds to defensive momentum as much as a quarterback sack.

—confusing blockers and resulting in quick tackles and a loss of yardage. However, a substantial number of times they can backfire, and the ball gets to the area vacated by the blitzing player. Since he is not there, a big gain of yards or even a score is likely. So stunts can work both ways, but more often they work very well for the defense.

Pass Defense

Hold the receivers; rush the passer; get the ball—the three keys to pass defense! It's unfortunate that it becomes such a low priority at the youth levels because there are far fewer passes. But against a passing team, and certainly in high school, pass defense fundamentals are essential to stopping the aerial game.

First, we must delay the receivers at the line of scrimmage for a step or two. Any delay in running their patterns will take precious time from the quarterback and add substantially to the pressure on him. Pressure on a quarterback will produce more errant passes than anything else.

The defensive end gives a shoulder or forearm to the offensive end to delay him. A cornerback shivers a wide receiver at the line of scrimmage for a second. A second is all that is needed. The defensive back can hit a receiver only in the first five yards and cannot touch him after that. It's also important *not to hold the receiver*, which is a serious penalty. However, it is helpful even if only by getting in his way we delay him for a step or two.

The second key is to pressure the passer. *If he gets four or five seconds to throw the ball, he will be able to pass at will.* Time gives receivers a real advantage to change direction, make fakes, and get free. When the defensive line sees a pass play developing (it becomes evident quickly that it is a pass play when the offensive linemen do not cross the line of scrimmage), they must engage in a furious and frantic penetration to the quarterback. *There is nothing more unsettling to a quarterback than to be under pressure.* Pressure is the best weapon against passing accuracy, and a quarterback sack will give a decided momentum to the defensive team. (See Figure 59.) Kids should be instructed to yell out "Pass!" as soon as they see it develop—this word should act as a lightning bolt to the defensive line to charge the passer. Just the sound of their frenzy will be upsetting to the passer.

Once the ball is in the air, *it is anybody's ball!* As long as the defender is going for the ball, he has as much right to it as the intended receiver. Therefore, once the ball is airborne, go for it. Forget the receiver if you have a chance to catch it. Otherwise, time your approach to slam the receiver as soon as he catches the ball. Anticipation is the defenseman's best friend. Lash at the ball to jar it free. If a teammate makes the interception, do not hesitate to block for him immediately.

OFFENSIVE FORMATIONS

At college and pro levels, and even at high school levels, a smart coach will use different offensive formations each week to exploit individual weaknesses in the opponent's defense or to maximize the abilities of his own talent. The difference in various offensive formations pertains primarily to how the running backs and receivers are positioned. Some formations favor the running play and some favor the pass. The interior linemen are nearly always lined up the same way and vary only in how close they are to each other. For instance, in a short yardage play or a punt, they line up very close to each other. However, the placement of the backs and receivers can vary greatly.

Figure 60 contains two formations that were very popular in the early days of football. The *single-wing* and the *T* are two of the oldest, but are not used much anymore. Both of these formations

Figure 60
EARLY FOOTBALL FORMATIONS

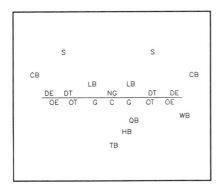 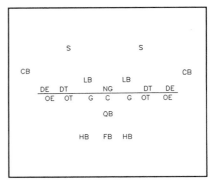

THE SINGLE-WING *In the single-wing the ball is hiked directly to a tailback or a half-back. The power is shifted entirely to one wing.*

THE T *In the T formation all backs are able to hit any hole or block for any other back. A pure and powerful running formation.*

are classic running or power formations and were used exclusively in the days before passing was allowed. In the deceptive T formation, the three running backs can strike any place on the line and can also block for each other. The ends stay in tight to block. The single-wing formation is even older than the T. It snaps the ball directly to a running back set 4 to 5 yards deep. The quarterback and a halfback are lined up to one side, with a wingback outside of the tight end.

The single-wing thus allows the offense to shift its strength to one side, adding greatly to the ability to run power plays to that side. Since this was before the rule requiring the offense to be set for a full second before the snap, the offense had a big advantage. However, the long snap created problems of its own, and so the T was introduced to have the quarterback take snaps directly. It also increased the number of potential running backs to three, and this provided the running game with more blocking and more flexibility.

Then came the day of the forward pass. It revolutionized the offensive formation. First came the *open formation*. It split one of the ends out wide along the line of scrimmage on one side and placed a flanker back out wide on the other side. The wide formation increases the chance for these receivers to face one-on-one coverage and spreads out the defense to the benefit of the running game. So the open formation posed a balanced threat for both the

Figure 61
COMBINED PASSING AND RUNNING FORMATIONS

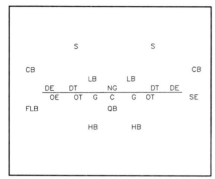

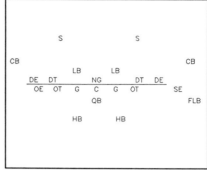

THE OPEN SET *In the open formation the defense is opened up for a balanced run or pass attack. Two backs are positioned to run or pass block and two receivers, a flanker, and a split end are wide for a pass.*

THE TWIN SET *The twin set is just like the open formation except that both wide receivers are on one side. This allows them to make moves off each other such as crossing patterns.*

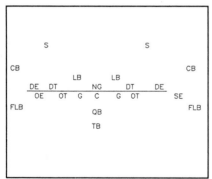

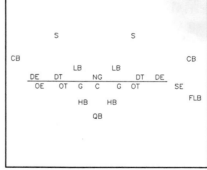

THE LONE SET BACK *This is one of the purest of passing formations and is used regularly in the pro's. There is one single set back and three wide receivers. A variation could line up all three receivers on one side in an I formation, thus overloading the protection on that side.*

THE SHOTGUN *The shotgun throws the ball back to the quarterback who can immediately focus on the pass pattern.*

Figure 62
MODERN YOUTH LEVEL FORMATIONS

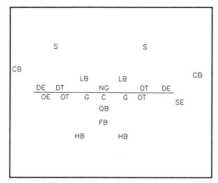 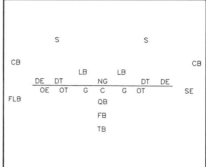

THE WISHBONE *This is a running formation much like the old T formation except that the fullback is pulled up closer to make the dive plays quicker and also block quicker.*

THE I *The I formation is much like the open formation as it allows for a balanced passing and running game. The I shape lineup helps to conceal the play and gives more power up the middle.*

run and the pass. (See Figure 61.)

Other formations came along over the years. The *twin set formation* placed both wide receivers on the same side, allowing them to work crossing and other patterns off each other. Finally, the ultimate passing formation, the *single back* or *lone set back*, came upon the scene, allowing for three wide receivers. Of course the lone running back has no other back to block for him, but some of the game's great running backs proved they could still get their yards, especially since the defense is so spread out to cover passes. The *shotgun formation* was popularized early on by the Dallas Cowboys. Here the quarterback takes the snap after lining up 5 yards behind center. Since it is quite awkward to hand off in this formation, it pretty clearly signals a pass. It helps the quarterback a lot since he can start looking at the defensive coverage right away, without having to back-pedal first. One or two backs are kept back to block in this formation.

In his early years of football, your son will not see many purely passing formations. There are, however, several good running formations used. Modern coaches still like to use split ends to take a cornerback out of the action and open up the defense a bit. We see the *wishbone formation* a lot at young ages. It provides much of the running power that we saw in the old T formation, except that the fullback plays forward a bit to better enable him to block and also to hit the hole more quickly on straight dive plays. The *I formation* is another popular one. It is like the open formation except that the fullback and a tailback are in a straight line behind the quarterback. (See Figure 62.) Sometimes, but rarely, a team will line up in an unbalanced line that serves to confuse the defense. If the defense does not shift in this case, the offense will have more players and thus more power to that side of the center.

There are other formations used and each coach has his own favorite. There are hundreds, perhaps thousands, of offensive plays that can be run from the various formations. The youth leagues are following the pro formations more and more. The *veer formation* is used sometimes. It's like a twin set formation except that the running backs line up wide, almost behind the tackles, to open things up more and make possible plays like the triple option.

Your son's coach will have his own formations and it will be your son's job to memorize them. *You can be helpful by quizzing your child on his plays.* Coaches get *very* irritated when kids forget plays, and I've seen it cost kids their starting positions. It takes some repetition to go over these plays, so you can be most helpful here. *Your son needs to know what every person should do on every play.* At young ages kids are often shifted around into different positions. A coach will make changes all season. If he calls on your son to change positions, and your son has no clue how to play the new position, he will lose an important opportunity. So it pays to understand the *concept behind* each play and what everybody else has to do. At the very least, linemen should know what other linemen must do, and so with backs.

Your child must approach each play from the standpoint of the *area he is to block.* The defensive formation on the play diagram, or the one he sees in practice, may change or the defense may be stunting. Usually at youth ages the defense comes with a five man line. In this defense the nose guard lines up on the offensive center, defensive tackles on the outside shoulder of offensive tackles, ends outside the offensive end, and linebackers on the guards. However, sometimes they will see a four man defensive line or a six man defensive line. Your child must understand that his assignment is to block *whomever* is in his area of responsibility when he gets there, and to block them away from the path of the ball-carrier. So, it stands to reason that he must also know where the ball-carrier is going. A more general understanding of the play will help him become more valuable since he can react to changing circumstances in light of a full understanding of the concept of the play.

OFFENSIVE PLAY PATTERNS

There are an endless number of possible offensive plays. They fall into general categories. The *gaps* between each offensive lineman are often numbered. (See Figure 63.) Some plays are coded in a way that includes these numbers; for instance, 143 would signify that the #4 back (usually a halfback) will carry through the #3 hole between the left guard and tackle. The first digit signifies a straight running play, as opposed to a draw. Nowadays, however, plays usually just have names.

Therefore, a *dive* is a run up the middle to either side of center into the #0 or #1 hole. A *slant* runs off-guard into the #2 or #3 hole. *Off-tackle* is another slant play into the #4 or #5 hole. An *end-around* goes to the #6 or #7 hole. The *sweep play* uses the #8 or #9 hole. Not all teams designate gaps with numbers. Some just use terms like dive, slant, belly, counter, or sweep. There are also *option plays* in which the quarterback runs wide with another running back on his outside shoulder. If a tackler approaches, the quarterback has the option of cutting inside or pitching the ball outside to the other runner. I've seen the *triple option play* in Pop Warner ball. Here the quarterback turns to hand the ball to the fullback. However, he rides the belly of the fullback and looks at the defensive tackle before releasing the ball. If the tackle commits himself forward, the quarterback releases the ball. If the tackle holds back, covering the zone, the quarterback takes the ball back and heads outside for a regular option pattern. More and more we see plays that give options depending on what the defense does *after the play starts*.

The series of diagrams in Figure 64 shows a number of play patterns that are useful from a wishbone offense, just to give you a feel for what your son will be expected to learn.

Figure 63
LINE GAPS

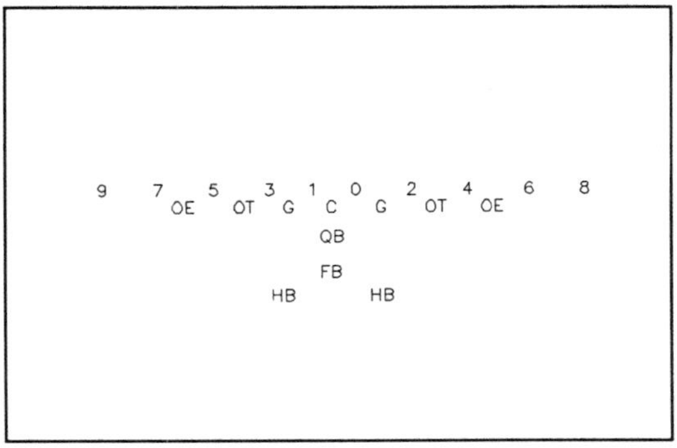

```
9   7   5   3   1   0   2   4   6   8
      OE  OT  G   C   G   OT  OE
                 QB
                 FB
            HB      HB
```

Your son's team may not assign numbers to gaps, but I always found it helpful to do so.

DEFENSIVE FORMATIONS

As mentioned before, the idea is to keep enough strength up the middle on defense to force the offense to run wide or pass. Success up the middle is critical to winning football. Usually a middle or inside linebacker is the most critical to defensive success. I've also seen good nose guards terrify the offense, cause mis-snaps and fumbles, unnerve the quarterback, and generally wreak havoc in the offensive backfield.

There are not as many defensive formations employed as there are offensive formations, particularly at the young ages. The standard defense is a five man line with two inside linebackers, two cornerbacks, and two deep safeties. The four man defensive line is more used in the pro's where there is more passing. (See Figure 65.) In short yardage situations a team will go to a six or seven man defensive line. The eight man gap defense is used on goal line situations. I prefer the five man line as a general defensive setup for kids. It seems to provide the general flexibility and balance needed for youth play.

Figure 64
OFFENSIVE PLAY PATTERNS

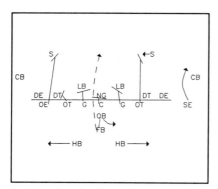

In this simple dive play the fullback powers into the line.

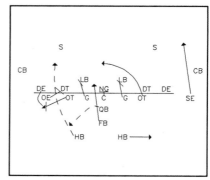

An off-tackle slant, cross block at the line, and fake to the fullback.

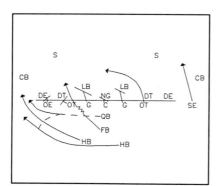

Here's a triple option—the quarterback, looking at what the defensive tackle does, bellies the fullback and then can sweep out with the option of using either halfback.

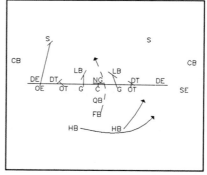

This is a counter-play to the fullback. The flow is to the right and he counters back to the left fullback.

Figure 64 cont'd
OFFENSIVE PLAY PATTERNS

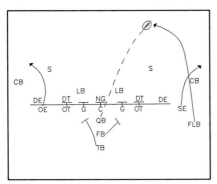

Here's a deep post pattern (to the goal post); it's also known as a Hail Mary or deep bomb.

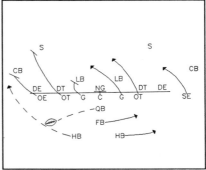

The pitchout is another favorite— the halfback just outruns everybody.

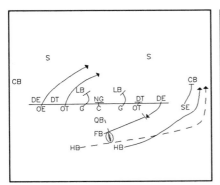

On a typical sweep play, everybody heads east and tries to get the halfback around the sideline.

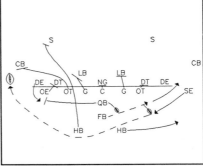

A little razzle-dazzle reverse to a quick split end can catch a defense that goes into pursuit too quickly.

Figure 65
DEFENSIVE FORMATIONS

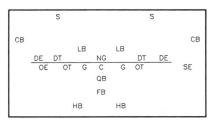

THE 54 *The standard defense at the youth level and you will see a lot of it. It's been called the Oklahoma 54. It nicely balances against the run and the pass and equally distributes individual defensive responsibility across the line with defenders generally hitting gaps.*

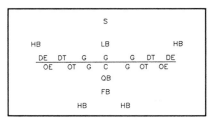

THE SEVEN DIAMOND *This is also called the seven gap since most linemen are in gaps. It's a short yardage defense with heavy responsibility on the halfbacks.*

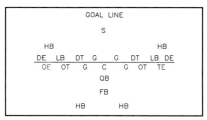

GOAL LINE *In this formation every gap is plugged, and the three defensive backs must assist by stopping the ball at the line.*

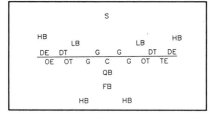

THE 62 *A six man line, stronger against the run than the 54, especially off-tackle.*

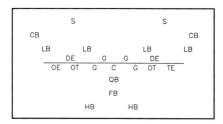

FOUR MAN LINE *In this formation every gap is plugged, and the three defensive backs must assist by stopping the ball at the line.*

6.

ODD AND ENDS

WORK WITH YOUR CHILD

As a parent, you should honestly evaluate your child's potential and desire. If he is a beginner, then the first objective is to learn the game fundamentals. Go over terminology and concepts. Talk about desire—the determination to overcome an opponent. Review the basic skill concepts behind blocking and tackling. Take him to a high school, college, or pro game. Start by promoting conditioning. Go out and have a catch. Get some advice on what position seems best suited for him and evaluate his relative speed. Encourage him to go out with his friends and play two-hand touch games. (In two-hand touch the idea is that a player is down when a defender touches him with both hands). Kids like to play tackle football, but without the protective equipment it makes no sense.

Review the main offensive and defensive concepts. Talk about each of the various positions. A local high school game is a great place to sit and review the fundamentals, watching as they actually occur in front of you.

As your child becomes a decent player, then you can help by concentrating on specific skills. If he is tall, give him practice receiving passes while you defend, but only aggressively enough to make it a challenge. Take some video shots (zoom in to the maximum) of his play, and review it with him. Don't harp on him or be too critical! Let him evaluate his own performance.

I think that it's most important to try to keep the game in perspective. There is already too much violence in society and it's easy for this sport to be associated with overly aggressive behavior. That can be most unfortunate, particularly if it turns your son into a bully of sorts. Try to emphasize the positive aspects, the character building, the development of courage, the growth of team spirit. In life we often get knocked down and then rise again to achieve. Football teaches life lessons. Discourage the degrading aspects.

BOYS AND GIRLS?

In my three prior books on parent coaching in baseball, soccer, and basketball, I studiously endeavored to assure gender neutral language. These sports are equally for both sexes. I have coached and played sports with both boys and girls.

However, this book is written in the masculine. It is merely a recognition of the obvious fact that extremely few girls play football. If you have a girl in the game, I apologize. I don't mean to exclude. However, it seemed senseless to write this book gender neutral since it is so very rare that girls play this sport.

I have no problem with girls playing football. At the very young ages girls and boys are very close in speed and aggressiveness and much closer in strength than in later years. They could clearly play the game. They rarely do. Perhaps it is the recognition that there is little future for them in the game. All-girl teams in high school are unheard of. Also, as I noted earlier, football is less about precision skills, which girls can achieve, and more about sheer strength, which Mother Nature has not given to many of them. Upper body strength is essential, and few girls have it.

While I would not recommend football as a choice for your daughter, she should never be denied the chance to try it. If she is gifted and determined, particularly at a young age, why not? I admire the girls who have done it under great media pressure, and perhaps someday it will grow as a women's sport. However, I doubt it.

CONDITIONING

Football is much more demanding of strength than most sports, certainly more than baseball, soccer, and basketball. It is not, however, an endurance sport, and kids can always find a moment to take a breather. Most coaches will concentrate on improving strength and toughness. However, jogging and wind sprints are always excellent conditioning and it never hurts to add them to your sessions, particularly wind sprints.

I rarely recommend weight training for youth sports, and I don't do so for football. A good calisthenic program is adequate. Push-ups are the best exercise since upper body strength is so very important to football. Tell your son to do fifty to one hundred per day. Your son will spend most of his time shoving another kid around, and the one with the strongest chest and shoulders will prevail. Chin-ups, as many as he can do, are also quite helpful. If you decide to allow some weight training and have a weight bench, then bench presses are probably the single best strength building method for football there is (not withstanding my reluctance to recommend weight training). Again, *upper body strength is crucial* and any help that you can give here will be immediately and quite noticeably rewarded on the field. I got my son a set of chest expanders, with springs attached to handles, and he used to do them while watching his silly cartoons. Rowing exercises are also very good to increase strength and stamina.

After the chest comes the legs. Partial squats, halfway bending the knee with some extra weight added, are quite good. Don't bend all the way. The long-standing tradition of running up stairs is excellent. Again, if you have a bench, the leg extender apparatus usually attached is also very good. Whenever using weights focus on strength conditioning. Use low weights with multiple repetitions. High weight just pumps up size and that's not needed, particularly at youth level play. Gentle neck exercises are also good, since the neck takes a pounding. Neck bridges are probably the best, but be careful not to overdo it here. Perhaps you can get a few pillows under the back to reduce the strain initially.

Muscles are like bubblegum. If you stretch gum quickly it tears or snaps, but if you stretch it slowly it expands nicely. Stretching before practice and games will help prevent muscles from tearing or snapping. No practice of any kind should begin without some slow jogging, some jumping jacks (for the ankles), and some general stretching (for the upper thigh, trunk, and neck). Running sideways and backwards or any agility exercises are quite good also.

INJURIES

No matter how well-conditioned a team is, injuries can occur anytime. A common injury is a hamstring pull, but these usually don't occur until high school or later. Strained knees, ankles, and necks are the most common to football. Upper leg (groin) strains, bloody noses, sprained wrists and forearms, jammed fingers, dislocations, and bruises also occur. Thankfully, broken bones are rare, but not rare enough. Most youth teams have trained first-aid people. I went through the program for my son's team and it was quite good. Ambulances are usually present at games, but not at practices, where many injuries occur.

Abrasions occur usually on the nose, although modern face gear protects the face much better than when I played. These are the most likely cuts to get infected. Wash the wound as soon as possible, with soap if it is handy. Apply a dressing when you are able to—the sooner the better! Just put some antiseptic on it. If it gets red, pussy, or red tracks appear, see a physician.

Lacerations are deeper wounds. Unless bleeding is severe, wash the wound and apply direct pressure with a bandage to stop the bleeding. If severe or deep, seek first aid. Keep applying pressure and secure the dressing with a bandage (you can tie the knot right over the wound to reinforce the pressure). Elevate the wound higher than the heart immediately to help slow the bleeding. Remember, if the bandage over the wound gets blood-soaked, never remove it; just apply a new dressing right over it. If the person has lost a lot of blood, you'll need to care for shock. Keep him warm with blankets and call for help. If a laceration is major, a butterfly bandage will hold the skin together. Consult a physician immediately for stitches.

Contusions and *bruises* occur frequently. Apply ice quickly after taking care of any abrasions or lacerations. Ice will arrest internal bleeding and prevent or lessen swelling. Ice is the best first aid available for nearly any swelling from bruises or sprains. Apply it very quickly—within minutes—and much internal damage will be spared. Do not move the child—especially if he is down due to a tough tackle or jolt. He could have a spinal injury and the slightest movement by an untrained person could do some serious damage.

Sprained ankles, knees, or wrists should be immobilized. An ice pack should be applied immediately. Act as if there is a fracture until you're sure there is no fracture. Call the ambulance if there is any question in your mind. Get an x-ray to see if there is a break or other damage.

If there is a *fracture*, immobilize the child completely as soon as possible. There should be no movement at all. Comfort him, get him warm with coats or blankets, and get medical help. Do not allow your child to be moved or cared for by anyone who is not medically trained.

If he is in the middle of the field during a championship game, the game can wait! Insist on this. Permanent damage can result from aggravating a break.

If your child ever falls to the ground unconscious, see if anyone present has been trained in first aid. The first move, once it is clear that the child will not respond, is to check for the vital signs—airway, breathing, and circulation, the ABC's of first aid. Send for an ambulance and let a trained person administer rescue breathing or CPR (cardio-pulmonary resuscitation), if necessary. Try to stay calm and let the first-aiders do their job. In all my years of coaching four sports and playing even more, I've never seen it needed. I hope that you won't either.

Finally, *heat exhaustion* can occur during football practices or games, particularly early in the season during those sweltering August practice sessions. The body gets clammy and pale. Remove the child from the playing field, apply cool towels, and elevate the feet. If the body temperature is very high and pupils are constricted, you should suspect heat stroke. Call an ambulance and cool him down fast. Care for shock.

Knees are tough injuries. Often the injury will require some sort of arthroscopic surgery to mend cartilage. Modern procedures are quite advanced, and simple. Have your child see a knowledgeable sports doctor. Your team's coach or high school athletic director will know one.

Tell your child to play the game safely. Aggressiveness is okay, but never intentionally hurt someone. Hope that other parents do the same. I play flag football frequently, and there are often one or two guys who take chances with the health of others. Don't encourage your child to grow up to be like them.

When an injury occurs, insist on rest. I've seen many kids rush back from a sprained ankle, only to have the injury plague them through the years. Don't let it happen! And make sure that your child wears an ankle brace from then on. There are excellent ankle braces on the market today. Get one.

The point is that injuries need time to heal right. If you give them that time, the future can have many years of sports for your child. If you don't, it could be over already.

IN THE STANDS

Well, football stands are loud places. The game seems to fire up everyone and so you will have to go with the flow. The noise is part of it all. Unfortunately, there are always a few super-screamers —parents who get out of control. They look quite foolish and are very irritating to sit near. It is as if they have been given a license to leave their senses. Sure, everyone cheers loudly on a big play, and sure, it is very helpful to get some noise going to get the teams pumped up, but don't be a spectacle and have some consideration for the other fans around you. Most important, be positive. Don't unduly criticize anyone, especially your own child. If you criticize another player, chances are his parents are nearby. What purpose does this type of outburst serve? Don't take out your frustrations on the kid when he makes a mistake. It embarrasses both of you, and it only teaches the child to play less confidently. I guarantee that they will all make mistakes, for years even, and they will not improve if you punctuate mistakes with things like "What's the matter with you?", "That was stupid!", or "If you don't get going, I'll . . ." That kind of talk is disastrous.

If you cannot control yourself, then stay home. This may sound tough, but you will do a lot of damage to your child and to your relationship with your child if you don't control your anger. Some people just can't keep it in, so avoid damage by staying home. I've seen this problem often, and it really can screw a kid up. If you must yell, then say things like "Tough D," "Stay Low," or "Let's Go." Congratulate a good effort. Let the coach call the plays.

HOW TO TREAT THE COACH

First of all, the coach is giving up a lot of time to coach the team and deserves a lot of room. If you want to coach, sign up to do so or to help. Show up at practices or at club meetings to offer help. That earns you the right to give an opinion. Otherwise, be very conservative about offering it.

Second, realize your bias. You are a parent and you love your son. You may think that he deserves to play more or to play another position, but the coach knows a lot more about what all the kids can do and who has earned playing time. It's unfair for you to ask for more and unfair to the other kids for you, in effect, to suggest that one of them should play less. Just work more with your child so that he improves, and he will play more. Coaches want to win, and they usually will give the better players more playing time.

However, coaches need to learn too. And sometimes they are going about things quite wrong. If this is the case, then gently indicate how you feel. It is important that you think about it a lot and make sure that you know what you are talking about before you say anything. Question your own bias. But if you feel that you can help, offer your opinion about it. Avoid an argument, or even a long debate. Make your point and ask the coach to think about it. Indicate that you are only trying to help. I would strongly suggest not being argumentative. Say your piece, listen to the coach, then thank him for his time and end it. If you are lucky, the coach will be thankful. However, he may resent your interference and possibly even take it out on your child. If the situation becomes very bad, let your club president or school athletic director know how you feel. But keep in mind that if your child gets in the middle of it, he may suffer for it. If the experience is more damaging than good, then remove your child from the team. But remember, think about it, get advice, talk to other parents, and avoid being unduly disruptive.

7.

PARENT'S CHECKLIST

Take this book, or at least photocopy these pages, when you go to watch your son at practice or a game. Look over the checkpoints one at a time and evaluate his performance. Make notes on paper or even write on the checklist what he may be doing wrong.

If you are a coach, bring it along to practice and look it over from time to time. It will help you to focus your attention on possible problem areas. Repetition of key phrases will help the player to concentrate on his basics. This checklist covers only basic skills.

DESIRE

- [ ] Ya gotta want it.
- [ ] Let's roughhouse.
- [ ] You are well-protected.
- [ ] Hustle; play the whistle.
- [ ] Never quit.

BLOCKING

Stance
- [ ] Drop sharply from ready to set positions.
- [ ] Set position—shoulder low and coiled.

- ❏ Legs shoulder-width or more apart.
- ❏ Weight moderately forward on hand.
- ❏ Down hand is inside back foot and just forward of shoulder, resting on the three interior fingers' knuckles, thumb back.
- ❏ Legs should be bent just enough so that the back is parallel to the ground.
- ❏ The tail should not be higher than the shoulders.
- ❏ The head should be up.
- ❏ The back should be straight, not curved.
- ❏ Bull the neck, eyes forward. Don't give away any clues.

Charge
- ❏ Explode instantly with the snap.
- ❏ Drive forward with the back foot.
- ❏ Stay low, legs wide, knees bent.
- ❏ Raise forearms toward opponent's chest, elbows out.
- ❏ Angle, don't step to opposite side.
- ❏ Adjust for stunts.

Jolt
- ❏ Slam shoulder into opponent *hard*.
- ❏ Drive, don't lunge.
- ❏ Straighten legs on contact.
- ❏ Keep eyes open wide, head up.
- ❏ Sustaining the block.
- ❏ Keep legs wide.
- ❏ Bring back leg up under the body.
- ❏ Move into the opponent's pressure.
- ❏ Drive forward with short, choppy steps.
- ❏ Turn opponent away and then back to scrimmage.

Specialty blocks
- ❏ Trap.
- ❏ Cross block.
- ❏ Body block.
- ❏ Double-team.
- ❏ Pass block.

TACKLING

Stance
- ❏ Similar to blocker, but more weight forward.

❏ Low under the opponent.
❏ Inside foot back.
❏ Search for clues.
❏ Crouch on standing stance.

Hit and hunt; shiver and shed
❏ Explode off the snap.
❏ Neutralize the blocker's charge with the shoulder (to penetrate) or shiver. Give a jolt of your own.
❏ Shiver. Both palms thrust up into opponent's shoulder pads to keep opponent at bay.
❏ Stay under control.
❏ Drop to all fours if not blocked. Stack things up.
❏ Shed or push blocker off at moment ball-carrier commits to one side.

Focus and wrap
❏ Drop or dip low.
❏ Focus on the belt.
❏ Legs wide and balanced.
❏ Drive shoulder into midsection. Jolt.
❏ Wrap arms tightly around the runner, try to smack the ball.
❏ Bring legs up quickly.
❏ Lift and then bring him down.
❏ If off-balance, tackle him any way possible.

PASSING

❏ A foundation of good form is essential under pressure.
❏ Size up the defense. Where are the seams?
❏ Secure the snap with passing hand on top, fingers spread.
❏ Retreat quickly. Practice the footwork.
❏ Hold the ball high.
❏ Step forward into pocket.

Grip
❏ Snug but not a squeeze.
❏ Fingers spread wide, touching ball along the entire length.
❏ Hand back of center. Pinky is mid-ball.
❏ Laces under last joint of fingers.
❏ Some space between palm and ball.
❏ Guide ball with free hand.

Release
- ❏ Stand erect, survey the field.
- ❏ Hold the ball high.
- ❏ Hit the player just as he breaks and is in a seam between defenders.
- ❏ Don't take too big a step. Step toward target.
- ❏ Snap the wrist, ball rolls off fingertips.
- ❏ Long pass. Tilt the nose up. Err long.
- ❏ Short pass. Nose even, snap and throw hard. Err low and short.
- ❏ Jump pass. Adjust lead, release at top of jump. Try to get some forward momentum.

RECEIVING

- ❏ Don't let the opponent delay you at the line.
- ❏ Run directly at the defender.
- ❏ Cut into pattern when he changes momentum to back-pedal.
- ❏ Make a two or three step fake and quickly change direction.
- ❏ Stay under control. Save a bit of speed.
- ❏ React to the ball.
- ❏ Don't ignore the passer. Look to him.
- ❏ Focus on the ball.
- ❏ Don't reach too soon.
- ❏ Soft hands, fingers curled and spread.
- ❏ Catch it high, at front point or tip of the ball.
- ❏ Watch the ball all the way into the hands.
- ❏ Try to catch the ball while body is in the air.
- ❏ Recover and tackle if intercepted.
- ❏ Tuck the ball in before running.
- ❏ Change direction immediately.

RUNNING

Stance
- ❏ Feet spread wide outside shoulders.
- ❏ Very little weight on down hand.
- ❏ Focus straight ahead. Don't tip off the defense.

Pivot and snap
- ❏ Pivot first before stepping.

❏ Snap head and shoulders.
❏ Push off balls of the feet.
❏ First step is large one with foot on same side as play action.
❏ Look at the hole to see what is developing and let the quarterback worry about getting you the ball.
❏ Outside arm down across stomach, palm up, and the other arm elbow up across the chest on dive plays.
❏ Curl both hands around the tips of the ball.
❏ Carry the ball securely. Jam it into the pocket between the upper arm and ribs, forearm to the underside, fingers spread around the front top.
❏ Carry the ball in the arm farthest from the tackler, usually the arm closest to the nearest sideline.
❏ Run with power; run hard.
❏ Running maneuvers.
❏ Stiff arm. Just as tackler launches, place palm on shoulder or on top of helmet, lock arm, hop on contact.
❏ Step out. Jab and then step or leap sharply away.
❏ Pivot or spin. Give a leg and take it away with 360 degree spin, changing direction.
❏ Cross over. Lean and lift leg away from tackler.

SPECIALTIES

Snap to quarterback
❏ Feet wide, hips high, legs even.
❏ Weight moderately on the ball.
❏ Head and arm may be in neutral zone.
❏ Tilt ball as needed.
❏ Timing is critical.
❏ Quick firm snap to the hands, laces to fingertips.
❏ Step forward with the snap.
❏ Angle head and jolt.

Snap for punts and place-kicks
❏ It's an upside down spiral pass.
❏ Hold ball up front with a passer's grip.
❏ Raise the front point of the ball.
❏ Weight forward moderately on the ball.
❏ Guide it with the left hand; this hand leaves the ball first.

❑ Brace and step forward with the snap.
❑ Drive ball back with quick snapping action.
❑ Aim for belt of the punter or hands of the place-kick holder.
❑ Snap with speed, time is precious. Take as little as possible.
❑ Focus on the snap, not the opponent.

Punting
❑ Look only at the ball as it is snapped.
❑ Feet parallel, weight on left foot.
❑ Arms extended outward, palms down and inward, thumbs up, fingers spread.
❑ Stand erect, hands soft, body relaxed.
❑ Let the snap come all the way to the hands.
❑ Withdraw and soften hands to receive the ball.
❑ Place the laces up; right hand back cradling the ball.
❑ Serve, don't drop ball to foot. Use right hand.
❑ Tip of ball points down and inside a bit.
❑ Spiral comes if ball is kicked with right side of instep, right side of shoelaces, just a hair off center. Contact on bottom belly of the ball.
❑ End over end kick if ball is kicked directly on the instep.
❑ Snap the locked ankle forward to give power and distance.
❑ Point the toe out.
❑ Concentrate on point of contact.
❑ Follow through enough to pull the body forward a hop.

Place-kicking
❑ Take two or three steps, depending on distance.
❑ Kick soccer style, using instep.
❑ Stand with legs nearly even, leaning forward on front foot while waiting for snap.
❑ Approach ball in a semi-circular motion.
❑ Plant toes of free foot even with back of ball, a few inches to the side, pointing at the target.
❑ Concentrate on point of contact.

Receiving punts and kickoffs.
❑ Judge where the ball will land.
❑ Catch it moving forward.
❑ Arms raised outward, upward a bit, palms up, fingers spread, hands fairly close together.
❑ Catch with hands and bring quickly into body.
❑ Soften hands and body for the catch.

Index

A

Abrasions, 130
Adornments, 87
Airways, 110-1
Attitude, 11-5, 62

B

Backfield, 61, 63, 87
Ball, 87
Ball possession, 106
Basic skills, 17-60
 blocking, 18-33
 passing, 38-46
 receiving, 46-50
 running, 50-6
 specialties, 56-60
 tackling, 33-8
Bat, 87
Bavaro, Mark, 66
Belly, 87
Blitz, 87-8
Block, sustaining,
 photo, 28
Block, trap, diagram,
 109
Blocking, 17, 18-33, 86,
 88, 107, 135-6
 charge, 24-7, 136
  photos, 25
 digging out, photo, 28
 illegal, 86
 jolt, 27-9, 136
  photo, 28
 legal, 86
 pass, 31-3
 photos, 19
 slant, 107
 specialty, 30-3, 136
 stance, 20-4, 135-6
  photos, 21, 23
 sustain, 29-30
Blocks, crab, 31, 66
Blocks, cross body, 31,
 66, 88
Blocks, open field, 33,
 88
Blocks, shoulder, 88
Blocks, specialty, 30-3,
 136

Blow, shiver, 31-3
Bomb, diagram, 125
Bootleg, 88
Brown, Jim, 50
Bruises, 130
Buck, 88
Buttonhook, 49, 88-9
 diagram, 88

C

Catching punts, 60
Center, 57, 63-5, 89
 photo, 64
Chain gang, 89
Charge, blocking, 24-7,
 136
 photos, 25
Charge, tackling,
 photos, 36
Checklist, parent's,
 135-40
Cheerleaders, 89
Clipping, 89
Coach, treating the,
 132-3
Concepts, 105-17
 defensive, 112-7
 offensive, 106-12
Conditioning, 128-9
Confidence, 15
Contusions, 130
Cornerbacks, 78
Counter, 89
Counter-play, diagram,
 124
Crab block, 31, 66
Cross body block, 31,
 66, 88
Cross-block, 30
Crossover, 56
Crouch stance, 34-5
Cutback, 89

D

Dead ball spot, 89
Defense, 89, 103, 116-7
 pass, 116-7
 zone, 103
Defensive backs, 78

Defensive concepts,
 112-7
Defensive end, 73, 74-5
 photo, 73
Defensive formations,
 123, 126
 diagrams, 126
Defensive line stance,
 34-5
Defensive positions,
 72-8
 backs, 78
 end, 74-5
 linebacker, 75-8
 nose guard, 72, 74
 tackle, 74
Defensive secondary,
 photos, 77
Defensive stance,
 photos, 32
Defensive tackle, 73, 74
 photo, 73
Desire, 9-15, 135
 photo, 10
Digging out, photo, 28
Dimensions of the field,
 diagram, 80
Dive, 37, 89-90, 122,
 124
 diagram, 124
 submarine, 37
Double-team, 31, 90
Down, 79-81, 90, 91
 first, 91
Draw play, 90, 108-10
 diagram, 109
Drills, passing, 46
Drills, receiving, 50
Drive, blocking, 29-30
Drop kick, 90
Dummy, 90

E

Encroachment, 85-6, 90
End, 61, 66-7, 73, 74-5,
 90
 defensive, 73, 74-5
  photo, 73
 split, 67

End, cont.
tight, 67
End-around, 122
End zone, 90
Equipment, 13, 90-1
illustration, 13
Exhaustion, heat, 131
Extra point, 91

F
Fair catch, 91
Faking, 47
False start, 84
Fear, 13-4
Field dimensions,
diagram, 80
Field goal, 91
Field measurements, 79
Field positions, 61-78
defensive, 72-8
diagram, 62
offensive, 63-72
54 formation, 126
First down, 91
Flag, 91
Flat, pass to the,
diagram, 113
Flea flicker, 91, 112
Focus and wrap,
tackling, 137
Formations, 105-6,
116-22, 123, 126
defensive, 123, 126
diagrams, 126
offensive, 116-22
Forward pass, 91
Forward progress, 91
Four man line
formation, 126
Four-point stance,
photo, 32
Fracture, 131
Free blocking zone, 83,
91-2
diagram, 83
Fullback, 68, 69-70, 92
photo, 68
Fumbles, 53, 92

G
Gaps, line, 92, 122, 123
diagram, 123
Girls, 128

Goal line, 92
Goal line formation,
126
Goal posts, 92
Grip, passing, 43, 137
photos, 43
Grip, running, 53-5
photos, 54
Guard, 64, 65-6, 92
photo, 64

H
Hail Mary, diagram,
125
Halfback, 68, 69, 92
photo, 68
Halftime, 92
Hand-off, 53
Hash marks, 92
Heat exhaustion, 131
Hit and hunt, 35-8, 137
Holding, 86
Holes, open, 106-7
photo, 107
Huddle, 92
Hunt, hit and, 35-8, 137

I
I formation, 120, 121
Illegal blocking, 86
Incompletion, 93
Ineligible receiver, 93
Injuries, 130-2
Interception, 93
Interference, 93

J
Jargon, 87-103
Jolt, blocking, 27-9, 136
photo, 28
Judge, line, 94
Jump passes, 45-6

K
Kick, drop, 90
Kickoff, 93, 140
photo, 93
receiving, 140

L
Lacerations, 130
Lateral, 93
Lead the play through
the hole, 107-8

Legal blocking, 86
Line, 61, 102-3
offensive, 61
unbalanced, 102-3
Line gaps, 122, 123
diagram, 123
Line judge, 94
Linebacker, 61, 75-8, 94
photo, 76
Linesman, 94
Lone set back
formation, 119, 120
diagram, 119
Long yardage, 108

M
Man-to-man, 94
Marks, hash, 92
Measurements of the
field, 79
Midfield, 94
Misdirection, 110
Mousetrap, 30
Moving the ball, 81-4
Muff, 94
Muscles, 129

N
National Federation of
State High School
Associations, 84
N.C.A.A., 38, 84
Neutral zone, 94
Nose guard, 71, 72, 74
photos, 71

O
Off-tackle, 94, 122, 124
diagram, 124
Offense, 94
Offensive concepts,
106-12
Offensive formations,
116-22
Offensive line, 61
Offensive play patterns,
122, 124-5
diagrams, 124-5
Offensive positions,
63-72
center, 63-5
ends, 66-7
fullbacks, 69-70

Offensive positions,
cont.
  guards, 64, 65-6
  halfbacks, 69
  quarterbacks, 70, 72
  tackles, 64, 66
  wide receiver, 67
Official signals,
  illustrations, 95-6
Officials, 94
Offside, 83, 84-5, 94
  photo, 83
Open field block, 33, 88
Open formation, 118
Open holes, 106-7
  photo, 107
Open set formation,
  diagram, 119
Option plays, 94, 112,
  122, 124
  triple, 94, 122, 124
  diagram, 124

P

Parent's checklist,
  135-40
Pass, forward, 91
Pass, screen, 100
Pass, timing, 102
Pass blocking, 31-3
Pass defense, 116-7
Passes, jump, 45-6
Passing, 38-46, 137-8
  drills, 46
  grip, 43, 137
    photos, 43
  release, 42-6, 138
  snap, photos, 40
  snap and retreat, 41-2
  wrist snap, photos, 44
Patterns, 105-6, 122,
  124-5
  offensive play, 122,
    124-5
  diagrams, 124-5
Payton, Walter, 50
Penalties, 97-8
Pile-up, 98, 99
  photo, 99
Pitchout, 98, 99, 125
  diagram, 125
  photo, 99

Pivot and snap, 51-3,
  138-9
  photo, 52
Place-kicking, 59, 60,
  98, 140
  photo, 59
Platoon, 98
Play patterns, offensive,
  122, 124-5
  diagrams, 124-5
Pocket, 98
Point after touchdown,
  98
Point, extra, 91
Pop Warner, 7, 85, 86,
  106
  age/weight chart, 85
Positions, field, 61-78
  diagram, 62
Positions, offensive,
  63-72
Possession, ball, 106
Post, 98
Post and wheel, photo,
  32
Post pattern, diagram,
  125
Power running play,
  106
Pressure the middle,
  114
Protection, 12-3
  illustration, 13
Pull, 30
Punter, 57
Punting, 58-60, 98, 100,
  140
  photos, 59
Punts, blocked, 58
Punts, catching, 60
Punts, receiving, 140
Pursuit, 100, 113, 114-5
  photo, 113

Q

Quarter, 100
Quarterback, 61-2, 68,
  70, 72, 100
  photo, 68
Quick slant pass,
  diagram, 113
Quitting, 14

R

Razzle-dazzle, 100,
  111-2, 125
  diagram, 125
Receiver, ineligible, 93
Receiver, wide, 67
Receiving, 46-50, 138,
  140
  drills, 50
  faking, 47
  photos, 48
  punts and kickoffs,
    140
Referee, 94
Release, pass, 42-6, 138
Replay, 100
Required equipment,
  illustration, 13
Retreat, snap and, 41-2
Reverse, 100, 112
Roll-out, 100
Roosevelt, Teddy, 38
Roughhouse, 10, 12
Rules, 84-7
Running, 50-6, 138-9
  crossover, 56
  grip, 53-5
    photos, 54
  hand-off, 53
  photos, 55
  pivot, 51-3
  snap, 51-3
  stance, 50-1, 52, 138
    photo, 52
  step-out, 56
  straight-arm, 56
Running back, photo,
  48

S

Sack, 100, 116
  photo, 116
Safety, 78, 100
Scoring, 82
Scramble, 100
Screen pass, 88, 100,
  111
Screening, 108, 110
Scrimmage, 100-1
Seam, 45
Secondary, 77, 101
  photos, 77

Seven diamond formation, 126
Shed, shiver and, 35-8, 137
  photos, 36
Shift, 101
Shiver, 31-3, 36, 101
  photos, 36
Shoestring tackle, 99, 101
  photo, 99
Short yardage, 108
Shotgun formation, 101, 119, 120
  diagram, 119
Shoulder blocks, 88
Sidelines, 101
Signals, official, 95-6, 101
  illustrations, 95-6
Simpson, O.J., 50
Single back formation, 120
Single-wing formation, 117-8
  diagram, 118
62 formation, 126
Skills, basic, 17-60
  blocking, 18-33
  passing, 38-46
  receiving, 46-50
  running, 50-6
  specialties, 56-60
  tackling, 33-8
Slant, 101, 107, 113, 122
  pass, quick, diagram, 113
Snap, 40, 57-8, 101, 139-40
  photos, 40
Snap, pivot and, 51-3, 138-9
  photo, 52
Snap, wrist, photos, 44
Specialties, 56-60, 139-40
  blocks, 30-3, 136
  catching punts, 60
  place-kicking, 60, 140
  punting, 58-60, 140
  receiving punts and kickoffs, 140
  snaps, 57-8, 139-40

Spin, 101
Spiral, 44
Split end, 67
Sprains, 130-1
Spread out the defense, 110
Stance, 20-4, 32, 34-5, 50-1, 52, 101, 135-7, 138
  blocking, 20-4, 135-6
    photos, 21, 23
  crouch, 34-5
  defensive, photos, 32
  defensive line, 34-5
  four-point, photo, 32
  running, 50-1, 52, 138
    photo, 52
  tackling, 136-7
  three-point, 22
Stands, in the, 132
Step-out, 56
Straight-arm, 56, 101
Stunts, 102, 115-6
  diagram, 115
Submarine dive, 37, 102
Substitution, 102
Sweep, 102, 109, 110, 122, 125
  diagram, 125
  photo, 109

T formation, 117-8, 121
  diagram, 118
Tackle, defensive, 73, 74, 102
  photo, 73
Tackle, offensive, 63, 64, 66
  photo, 64
Tackle, shoestring, 99, 101
  photo, 99
Tackling, 17, 33-8, 136-7
  focus and wrap, 137
  hit and hunt, 137
  photos, 39
  shiver and shed, 137
  stance, 137
Tailback, 102
Taylor, Lawrence, 75

Three-point stance, 22
Tight end, 67
Time out, 102
Timing pass, 102
Touchback, 102
Touchdown, 82, 102, 103
  photo, 103
Training, weight, 129
Trap, 30
Trap block, diagram, 109
Trapping, 102
Triple option, 94, 122, 124
  diagram, 124
Turn, blocking, 29-30
Turnovers, 38
Twin set formation, 119, 120
  diagram, 119

U
Umpire, 94
Unbalanced line, 102-3
Unconscious, 131

V
Veer formation, 121
Video tapes, 18

W
Waterboy, 103
Weight training, 129
Whistle, 13-4
Wide receiver, 67
Wingback, 103
Wishbone formation, 120, 121
Wrap, focus and, 137
Wrist snap, passing, photos, 44

Y
Yardage, long, 108
Yardage, short, 108

Z
Zone, end, 90
Zone, free blocking, 83, 91-2
  diagram, 83
Zone, neutral, 94
Zone defense, 103